THE 7 WORST THINGS PARENTS DO

John C. Friel, Ph.D.
Linda D. Friel, M.A.

Health Communications, Inc.
Deerfield Beach, Florida

www.hci-online.com

Library of Congress Cataloging-in-Publication Data

Friel, John C.
  The 7 worst things parents do/John C. Friel, Linda D. Friel.
    p. cm.
  Includes bibliographical references and index.
  ISBN 1-55874-668-4 (trade paper)
  1. Parenting.   2. Parents—Attitudes.   3. Parenting—Psychological
aspects. 4. Parent and child. 5. Child rearing. I. Friel, Linda D. II. Title.
III. Title: Seven worst things parents do.
  HQ755.8.F75 1999
  649'.1—dc21   98-52824
                                                                      CIP

©1999 John Friel and Linda Friel
ISBN 1-55874-668-4

Publisher: Health Communications, Inc.
             3201 S.W. 15th Street
             Deerfield Beach, FL 33442-8190

Cover illustrations by Lisa Camp

To all parents

Other Books by the Authors

Adult Children: The Secrets of Dysfunctional Families

An Adult Child's Guide to What's "Normal"

The Grown-Up Man: Heroes, Healing, Honor,
Hurt, Hope

Rescuing Your Spirit

The Soul of Adulthood: Opening the Doors

CONTENTS

Part III: Go for It

ACKNOWLEDGMENTS

We were about a fourth of the way through writing an entirely different book when our good friend and Clearlife/Lifeworks Clinic co-therapist, Mary Pietrini, suggested we write a parenting book based on all of the pertinent lecture material that she had heard during various clinic lectures over the past fourteen years. We have been working on it in our spare time ever since. We would like to thank Mary for working with us for so many years, and for knowing us and our work well enough to come up with that suggestion off the top of her head.

We would also like to thank James Maddock, Ph.D., University of Minnesota professor and clinical psychologist in private practice, for mentoring us over the many years that we have had the honor of knowing him. It is surely understatement to say that his competence, wisdom and professional integrity as both psychotherapist and teacher are remarkable. We especially appreciate the general comments that he made after reading one of the later drafts of this book.

We want to thank all of the individuals, couples and families with whom we have had the honor to work over the years in our private practice in Minnesota, as well as all of the people who have attended our seminars and workshops on both sides of the Atlantic. The opportunity to present and discuss our ideas in a public format has served to keep us informed, refreshed and challenged. Thanks also to all those who have attended one of our three-and-a-half day Clearlife/Lifeworks Clinics. We want to be sure to thank all of you who took what must have felt like a big risk to attend one of these, searching for your path to move forward.

Of course, we want to thank Peter Vegso, publisher and owner of Health Communications, for his continued interest in and support of our work; and our editor Matthew Diener, for his wise and competent management of this project; and Erica Orloff, for her comprehensive and exhaustive editing and suggestions for improvement of this book.

WARNING/DISCLAIMER

This book was written to help families who are having certain kinds of problems. Much of the material contained in this book is aimed at families who are in crisis or on the verge of crisis, but may not be aware of it. For example, some children's lack of impulse control and sense of personal responsibility has led mental health experts around the nation to grow increasingly concerned, as evidenced almost weekly by articles and programs in the media. For that reason, we wrote this book differently than our previous ones. This book was designed to hopefully provoke you into thinking and taking a closer look at these seven parenting mistakes.

We recognize that it takes a certain amount of money to make certain mistakes, such as always bailing out your children when they get into financial distress. At the same time, much of the material in this book is applicable, in one way or another, to all families. You will probably encounter examples in our book that do not apply to you for various reasons, and in those cases, we invite you to either extrapolate to your own situation, or ignore the example altogether. When we say, for example, that people often work themselves to death because of an uncontrolled need to acquire things, we also know full well that many families at the lower end of the economic continuum may be working a lot just to survive. If you fit in the latter category, we ask that you understand that we are not referring to you.

More important is the fact that these seven mistakes are not the worst things parents can do. Beating, torturing or sexually abusing children are by far worse than these. We hope this is obvious to all of our readers. We decided upon this title because we encounter many parents who believe they are doing a great job because they *aren't* torturing their children. In many cases, nothing could be further from the truth.

Please keep this in mind as you read our book.

Part I
Get Ready

1

The Seven Worst Things
Parents Do

"**W**hat could turn intelligent, independent-minded adults into virtual wimps?"

Barbara Walters asked this question at the beginning of a recent ABC News *20/20* segment about small children tyrannically controlling their parents. During this valuable piece of television journalism, viewers were subjected to videotaped scenes of a mother climbing in and out of bed with her little child. For several hours, the child manipulated the mother, bargained, sabotaged and pretty much ran the show, and Mom just kept playing the game. We watched another child who had a whole cup filled with toothbrushes in an obviously failed attempt to get the child to brush his teeth by giving him "choices." We watched a

3

child whine about wanting a can of soda with breakfast. Her mother said "no," but her father almost immediately turned around and gave the soda to his daughter "to keep peace." It's hard enough to watch these painful examples of well-intentioned parents trying methods that seem logical on the surface—but don't work. It is even harder to watch children who, if allowed to continue running the show, will be psychiatric basket cases by the time they reach adulthood.

A Family in Trouble

Eric and Pamela first approached us during a break at a seminar we were presenting. They wanted to know how to handle what they described as a normal problem their son was having. They seemed appropriately tentative about how much detail to offer, saying that he was a little resistant to brushing his teeth twice a day. We responded with an answer that matched the detail we were given; they seemed satisfied with the answer, and we moved on to the next person in line.

Eight weeks later, we noticed a new appointment in our book for an Eric and Pamela Jamison. When we greeted them at their first appointment, we recognized them as the couple who had asked the question several weeks before. Bobby, their five-year-old son, indeed resisted brushing his teeth on a regular basis, but that was just the tip of the iceberg. He also threw tantrums whenever he didn't get his way. Subsequent systematic measurement indicated that he was having as many as four major tantrums per day. He typically refused to eat what Pamela prepared for dinner, demanding something different, and then refusing to eat *that* after Pamela had gone out of her way to prepare it just for him. Bedtime was a nightmare that was causing an increasingly dangerous rift between Eric and Pamela, and mornings before work were so stressful that Eric was seriously thinking of moving out for fear that he might do something harmful to Bobby.

And there was more. Much more. But as we listened to their family structure unfold, what struck us most was the family's lack of definition. We were witnessing a family that had been unraveling for months and was now on the verge of despair. We told Eric and Pamela the following:

1. "We admire you. It takes a lot of courage and wisdom to admit you have a problem and seek help for it."

2. "You obviously love Bobby a great deal."

3. "Your overall goals for raising Bobby are excellent: You want the best for him; you want him to grow up to feel loved; you want him to become a warm and caring person; you want him to be able to actualize his God-given potentials; and you want him to become emotionally, socially and intellectually competent. These are admirable goals."

4. "It appears that some of the more specific methods that you have learned for achieving those goals are not working for you and Bobby. In our therapy sessions, we will try to give you some different tools that may work better."

We will continue with this family's story, and their successful resolution of their problem, in chapter 11.

Seven of the Worst Parenting Errors

Raising children is by far the most rewarding and daunting experience any human being can have. We say this from our own experience as well as that of the many people with whom we have worked. Raising children puts tremendous strain on a couple's emotional, financial, intellectual, spiritual and physical resources. Not surprisingly, research on marital happiness shows that couples are most satisfied with their marriages before the first child is born and after the last child leaves home. We therefore greatly respect those who currently engage in the daily tasks of leading their offspring from infancy into the independent adulthood that is the ultimate goal of parenting.

Parents who search for books of wisdom on childrearing will discover a bewildering, nearly infinite array of titles on the subject, which suggests that we are more confused and concerned about how to raise our children than almost anything else in the universe. Despite their confusion and lack of confidence, the majority of parents care about what happens to their children. And this is good. As we are catapulted into the twenty-first century, along with our laptop computers, Internet connections, cellular phones, faxes, pagers, digital video disc players, five hundred channels of cable television and the ever-present CNN news instantaneously informing us of major happenings around our tiny planet, it is incredibly important that people continue to care about the basics of life.

Which brings us to the origins and purpose of this little book. We have been psychologists for a long time and are continually grateful for the work that we are able to do. Some people are grateful for their artistic talents, some for their business acumen and some for their scientific wisdom. We are grateful for the daily opportunities we have to work with people who choose to struggle. We do not find it boring. We do not go home at night feeling drained and empty. And contrary to what you might already be thinking about us based on the title of this book, we by no means believe that we have all the "right" answers for people. But we do have many years of experience helping people work through their problems, and as a result, we have formulated some fairly clear opinions about what works and what doesn't, for many people.

We have also been around this field long enough to know that the instant anyone suggests a universal rule for child-rearing, an exception will appear somewhere, giving us all cause for great humility. On the one hand, life is much too awesome, mysterious and complex to be reduced to a simple formula. On the other hand, without principles and guidelines for living, we become little more than wild animals prowling the earth in search of our next meal, ready to kill anyone who gets in the way of our quest. This is one of the paradoxes of living— too many rules and guidelines squeeze the life right out of us, while too few result in life-threatening chaos.

With the above considerations in mind, we set out with the limited goal of sharing with you seven of the most important parenting considerations that we have identified over the years. The list is by no means conclusive. And we are well aware that some of these items will not apply to you; for some people, none of them will apply. As with the other books we have written, all we ask is that you give this material a chance—grapple with a particular concept a little bit rather than reject it out of hand. While we don't claim to have all the right answers, you may just find that some of the pain you experience as a parent is at least partly caused by one of these seven parenting errors. So here they are. Each one is a chapter in this book. We hope they challenge you.

1. Baby your child
2. Put your marriage last
3. Push your child into too many activities
4. Ignore your emotional or spiritual life
5. Be your child's best friend
6. Fail to give your child structure
7. Expect your child to fulfill *your* dreams

2

The Rules of the Game

It's pretty hard to succeed at the game if you don't know the rules, so this chapter explores the rules of the parenting game. There are other rules, too, but this chapter contains enough to get you headed in the right direction. Children and parents do better with clear structure. If you consistently flub the changes you try to institute in your home, have hope. It takes practice for everyone to become a good parent. Then simply return to this chapter and read it. Remember that sometimes people confuse "tried and true" with "true but trite." You may already know the "right" thing to do, and lost sight of it in your search for a more glamorous answer.

Small Changes Yield Big Results

One change instituted consistently can turn an entire system around. Think about one of our space probes just leaving Earth's orbit on its way to Jupiter. Imagine it is off-course by a fraction of a degree. Now, imagine mission control officials are unable to correct this tiny error midcourse because of a malfunction in the probe's thrusters. Lastly, imagine where the probe will be, several years later, when it is supposed to be entering Jupiter's atmosphere. It will be millions of miles off-course by then. Small changes yield big results.

Sometimes people enter therapy looking for high drama and quick fixes. Sometimes people seek the magic bullet that will change their entire family system overnight. In so doing, people miss the fact that one small change, maintained consistently and with integrity, can indeed change an entire system. Of course, systemic change won't happen overnight, no matter what you do. It takes time.

We suggest that people visualize a dial with a 360-degree scale on it and with a strong spring inside that tries to keep the dial at zero degrees. Imagine cranking that dial clockwise 270 degrees and then letting the dial quickly spring back. This is the picture of what often happens when we want to change too many things all at once. Our intentions are right but long-term change needs time to secure its position.

Now imagine turning that dial seven degrees and holding it there for twelve months despite the strong spring inside the dial that is trying to pull it back to zero. After twelve months of working diligently to keep it at seven degrees, you let go of the dial and find that it stays at seven degrees—the spring inside has adjusted to the new setting. Furthermore, you discover that many other aspects of your life have changed in important ways because of the internal growth that took place as you chose to work patiently to achieve this success instead of going for the quick fix.

Dysfunction Usually Equals Extremes

The opposite of dysfunctional is dysfunctional. Here are some common examples of extremes that tend to be equally dysfunctional in ways that are opposite, at least on the surface.

1. People who are clingy, helpless and whiny versus people who deny their own dependency needs and are therefore overly independent and need-less.

2. People who rage and knock holes in walls versus people who rage by pouting silently for two days to punish you.

3. People who never cry versus people who seem constantly tearful.

4. People who set way too many limits for their children versus those who are way too permissive.

5. Families where people spend almost no time together as a family versus families where people spend almost all their time together to the exclusion of outside relationships and interests.

6. People who have very rigid belief systems versus people who have lax or non-existent belief systems.

Struggle Is Good

Struggle is good. Without it we would not be alive. We would have no reason to exist. We would have no sense of accomplishment. The only time in our brief lives when we don't have to struggle is when we are in our mother's womb. But with birth and *labor,* our struggle begins. When parents try to remove all of the roadblocks from their children's paths they end up creating a fantasy world and an emotional prison for their children. If home is the only place on earth where the child has no struggle, and the child hasn't learned to appreciate struggle in the first place, then he won't leave home. He can't leave home. It's a setup for disappointment. Even if he leaves home physically, he'll never grow up and leave emotionally. Given these circumstances, why should he?

You Can't Change What You Aren't Willing to Admit, and What You Don't Admit Tends to Run the Show

If your home is in chaos, your children are out of control, you secretly resent your spouse for siding with the kids all the time, and you fantasize about running away to a remote tropical island, but you aren't willing to admit any of these feelings to anyone, including yourself, then you surely aren't likely to change any of these things. If you won't admit that there's a problem then how can you possibly fix it? And if you won't get the feelings out in the open, whatever isn't discussed and talked out tends to get acted out. Saying that you feel like running away isn't the end of the world. Waiting until you do run away may be the end of the healthy world for you.

Your Children Won't Break If You Let Them Grow Up

This should probably be a corollary to "struggle is good," but the inner fear that our children will break if they have to struggle is so real and so powerful for some parents that we thought we'd say it again in a different way. If you were spoiled, smothered and coddled as a child, or at the other extreme, if you were abused and neglected as a child, you may be at risk for believing that your children will break if you let them grow up. Of course, children are incredibly resilient, and in these cases we recommend that parents address their own childhood shortages rather than projecting them onto their kids. Being a parent is so much easier when we aren't unconsciously controlled by the ghosts of our own pasts.

A Few Rules, Enforced Consistently and Without Abuse, Are Superior to a Lot of Rules Enforced Inconsistently

This, in some ways, is a partial corollary to "small changes yield big results." Striking a balance is the goal here. When we see parents trying to enforce scores of itty-bitty rules, we know we are witnessing parents who are desperate in some way. If they are actually able to achieve compliance from their children with these scores of rules, which is a near-impossibility, it often means that the parents are extremely rigid, and often frightening to their children. Likewise, if we see parents who have too few rules, but who enforce them inconsistently, we know there are going to be problems.

For children, basic manners, a consistent bedtime with bedtime rituals such as a bath and brushing their teeth, a couple of regular chores that are done with consistency, and one or two other rules are really enough if those rules are enforced consistently. The only way children learn to have internal structure is by starting with external structure. Children who grow up with limits they can depend on, for example, a regular bedtime, will develop a clear internal structure that will serve them a lifetime. Something this simple may not seem like a big deal, but without a doubt it is a big deal.

Incompetent Children Cannot Have High Self-Esteem

Somewhere on the way to the twenty-first century, some adults got the idea that constantly praising children for every little thing they do will ultimately produce high self-esteem. This was probably in reaction to the harsh, shaming practices prior to this "self-esteem movement," but we need to get back on course. The opposite of dysfunctional is still dysfunctional. Of course we need to praise our children when they do things well. But we also need to let them struggle with problems by themselves and sometimes get their reward from the fact that they solved a problem on their own.

We need to teach our kids about life. It isn't enough to pump them up with empty praise for a job poorly done. We need to guide, teach, gently correct and help our kids move toward competence. Self-esteem, after all, comes from competence, not from incompetence. We have never met a human being who did not have something to offer the world. Our job as parents is to help our children discover their own gifts and then learn to do them well.

Our Unhealthy Behaviors Always Have Reasons and Payoffs (Otherwise We Wouldn't Engage in Them)

This is a corollary to "You can't change what you aren't willing to admit." We must be honest about the reasons for our unhealthy behaviors. All human behavior is motivated by something. We don't do things without a reason. Why would someone drink herself to death? Because the pain of dying from alcoholism does not seem as awful as the pain of living sober. Why would someone let his kids stay up 'til all hours of the night rather than enforcing a consistent bedtime? Because he wants to be liked, to be seen as "the good guy." Or because the guilt he would feel if he did enforce the bedtime seems more painful than the consequences of letting them stay up. Why would someone share her personal marital problems with her children rather than with her husband or other adults? Because children are vulnerable, accepting, need parents, are a captive audience, and because talking with other adults is scarier than sharing that information with children.

Life Is Not a Test, It's an Experiment— So Give New Things a Try

Above all, please remember that there are no perfect children, families or parents. No one is going to grade you on your parenting skills. No one is keeping score. You don't have to do it perfectly. You can't do it perfectly. You will make mistakes. Some of these will lead to temporary heartaches, but heartache is a necessary and deepening part of life. Nobody gets through parenting without some pain. Accept this truth, and you will find being a good parent much easier. It's true, and it's worth it.

Part II
The Seven

3

Baby Your Child

Babying Our Babies

In *Emotional Intelligence: Why It Can Matter More Than IQ,* Daniel Goleman cited Jerome Kagan's research on children who are innately, biologically timid. Mothers who protected their timid children from upsetting experiences produced kids who continued to be plagued by fear as they grew older. Mothers who gradually and consistently encouraged their kids to deal with more and more of the world produced children who were much less fearful later on. This outcome challenges the thinking of many contemporary American parents who believe that children should be shielded from life's difficulties. To the contrary, even biologically fearful children do better if their parents encourage them to conquer their fears.

"Infantilize" is a psychiatric term that means what you probably think it means—a less technical word would be to "baby" our children. With the apparent epidemic of parental neglect and family fragmentation occurring in the United States today, you might think that this is hardly a problem. But nothing could be further from the truth. For many reasons, a large number of American children can barely write a complete sentence let alone a five-page typed essay with correct grammar and punctuation. Many leave home in their early-twenties unable to run a washer and dryer, fry an egg, iron a shirt or blouse or reconcile a checkbook. And an alarming number of males between the ages of twenty-five and twenty-eight—estimates go as high as 30 percent—currently live at home in this country, and many of them pay no rent and do no chores around the house.

Back in the 1970s when we were supervising students in a university preschool, we noticed a disturbing trend. When faced with an activity such as drawing pictures or working with crafts, some of the little three- and four-year-old children who attended the preschool would work for a few moments and then just stop, apparently waiting to be praised for each line that they drew. As the school year progressed we realized that these children's parents had, with good intentions, gone overboard with suggestions from the self-esteem movement. Not wanting their children's self-esteem to be damaged, they had unconsciously decided that the best approach was to reward every little accomplishment achieved by their children. Of course, this kind of indiscriminate use of reinforcement actually has the opposite effect, making children so dependent on outside reward that they are virtually helpless on their own, ultimately lowering self-esteem to perilous levels. In *Smart Parenting: How to Parent so Children Will Learn*, nationally recognized parenting expert Dr. Sylvia Rimm wrote of the power wielded by children who are too dependent as a result of overprotection: "Because they are kind and caring and the children's symptoms of power (tears and requests for pity) are very persuasive, parents and teachers continue to protect them, unintentionally stealing from them their opportunities to cope with challenge." (p. 17)

But the parents meant well, didn't they? They certainly did. Parents have a hard job without much formal training to do it. But despite good intentions, rewarding children for every little action simply doesn't help. It paralyzes children, robbing them of the joys of struggle and accomplishment. In the 1960s, Stanford psychologist Walter Mischel conducted some groundbreaking research on delay of gratification in children. He discovered that four-year-olds who took a few marshmallows as soon as they were offered turned out to be remarkably different much later in life than those who chose to wait a few extra minutes to get more marshmallows. As teens, those who were able to delay gratification were still much better able to wait for things, but they were also much higher achievers, better adjusted socially and emotionally, got into much less trouble, were liked a lot more, and were a lot happier than teens who chose not to wait for more marshmallows when they were four. Mischel's findings are remarkable.

Optimal Doses of Struggle

Television news specials and inspirational books such as the *Chicken Soup for the Soul* series are filled with stories of extraordinary courage, perseverance, faith and hope. Sometimes we hear these stories and just shake our heads, muttering to ourselves that we could never display such courage or persistence. Or we wish we could but don't know how it's done. Part of the reason that some of us view these tales as filled with mystery is that the human spirit is sometimes unfathomable. But sometimes, we view these stories as incomprehensible because we weren't given *optimal doses of struggle* when we were growing up.

This is not a new concept. It's been around for a few thousand years at least. Erik Erikson, one of the fathers of modern personality theory, and one of the most respected psychologists of the twentieth century, addressed this question at least fifty years ago. Erikson coined the term "identity crisis," and in his neo-Freudian musings, he devised the eight stages of development, which begin in infancy with the trust versus mistrust crisis. If you read his original works, you will notice that successfully resolving each stage or crisis requires a balance between the urges and impulses of the developing child and the structure provided by parents. This dynamic balance creates a healthy struggle, and through this struggle, people grow up to be healthy. From birth to about eighteen months, infants' needs must be met with consistency so they realize that they are going to make it, and that they can rely on—that is, trust—their environment. But in the latter months of this stage, perhaps from twelve to eighteen months, it is also important for some of the infants' needs to *not* be met immediately. When babies have to wait a while for things, they learn two very important facts about life:

1. That they are separate from the people who are raising them
2. That they can't always get what they want

That latter one may sound familiar because it represents the beginnings of learning to delay gratification. If it's so simple and straightforward, why do so many of us have problems raising our kids? First, as parents we tend to:

1. Do what was done to us, or
2. Do the opposite of what was done to us

If what was done to us wasn't good, such as being parented with too rigid of a structure with too many rules and regulations, we will either repeat that pattern, or do the opposite—we'll create little structure at all for our kids—which is just as bad.

Second, many of us feel so guilty about what we're doing as parents that we try to make up for our mistakes in one area by being too permissive in another. Have you been fighting with your wife? Are you divorced? Do you spend all your time at work? Well, at least you let your kids eat junk food and watch all the television they want. That should make up for some of the pain they've experienced, right? Wrong. It just heaps pain on top of pain, compounding the problems like interest in a savings account.

Believe it or not, repairing the problem is easier than you

think. Look around you. Do you really like adults who are whiny, who can't wait for anything, and who are rude and demanding? How do you think they got that way? Erikson's work suggests that their parents either overcontrolled them or indulged them as children. Now look at your four-year-old. Does she whine a lot? Does she refuse to go to bed at her normal bedtime? Does she throw food, refuse to eat and cry at the drop of a hat? Do you secretly, and with terrible guilt, tell yourself that you've created a monster? Okay. You have a problem. Is it insurmountable? No problem is insurmountable and certainly not at age four. If you wait until age twenty-four, though, you may have created a long-term problem. And you may have a grown-up living with you just when you thought you were going to be able to enjoy your empty nest.

Struggle Is Good

In our last book, *The Soul of Adulthood,* we devoted an entire chapter to the key psychological truth that struggle is good. And then we devoted another entire chapter to the truth that resistance is good. It would be easy to write an entire book devoted to the idea that struggle and resistance are good. When our children don't have to struggle, they never grow up. Because life's journey provides an ample amount of resistance, a person who lacks the capacity to struggle and to experience joy and satisfaction while doing it will find life cruel and depressing. This is unfortunate because people who have learned how to struggle often find life challenging and exciting.

What to Do Instead

Identify the Problem

Begin with courage, honor, determination and a resolute spirit. Are your kids running the show? Have you inadvertently created little people who are miserable inside but so intoxicated with power that they can't let it go? They didn't do anything wrong. It's not their fault. They weren't put on earth to raise you. They didn't make the family rules. You did! Children are much happier and healthier when they have limits and structure. We put men on the moon and roving cameras on Mars so we know we can conquer this parenting problem. We know we can do it without being abusive, too.

Kids Who've Been Infantilized

Do you do everything for your children? Do you run behind them, ruining your back muscles as you bend over to catch them should they fall on their rear ends while they're learning to walk? You're doing exactly the same thing when they're twenty-one and you pay off their credit card debts for them, or get your attorney friend to get them off from a drunk driving charge when you know darned well they were driving drunk. We all mean well. But tying your children's shoes because you believe it's too much for them to handle is a dangerous precedent to set. And once set, it is hard to change. Tie his shoes today. Do her homework for her when she's nine. Rush in, make a big stink and save him every time he has a minor altercation with a peer. When she's twenty-four and struggling to make friends because she's always been sort of withdrawn, become her best friend so that she won't have to struggle, and then she won't ever grow up.

To not infantilize kids is an especially painful struggle for parents who grew up in adverse circumstances such as poverty or alcoholism, for obvious reasons. When we've had a rough time ourselves, we want to make sure that our kids don't have a rough time also. This causes us to develop blinders about certain aspects of life and it is these blinders that we must gently dismantle if we are to become competent parents and find balance in our lives. So sit down, alone, where it is quiet and there are no distractions, and listen to what your senses and your heart are telling you. Parents who work on this stuff diligently sooner or later tell us that a little voice inside of them was telling them they were infantilizing their children, but the voice had been drowned out by the terrible noise of their own painful childhoods.

It takes extraordinary courage, unimaginable dignity and incredible determination to listen to that small voice over the roar of the old hurts. And in every single case, when people listen to it, they are rewarded beyond their wildest expectations.

Kids Running the Show

What to look for? That is the question. In infancy, notice whether your sixteen-month-old is able to wait a few minutes, without having a major blowup, before you pick him up. What about bedtime? If you're raising your children with a few rules that are consistently enforced, then this should hardly ever be a problem. Kids feel much safer and are much healthier when there is a regular rhythm to their lives.

In general, children ought to be doing a few simple daily routines without a fuss. These include getting ready for bed, going to bed without coming out for something every few minutes, getting ready in the morning and putting their toys away at the end of the day. These may not seem important in a world that has become mind-bogglingly complex, but they are. Many parents say, "We don't emphasize bedtimes and chores because we'd rather see our kids staying up a little later and learning how to use their computers. If they don't learn that, they'll never succeed!" Rethink this. The more complex the world becomes, the more important routines like these are. Routines help create an inner structure and the ego-boundaries in children which are the very things that will distinguish the competent from the incompetent when they reach adulthood.

Define and Measure the Problem

Infantilizing

Sometimes the best general measures of infantilizing are, as previously described, things like your children still living at home at age twenty-six, four-year-olds who can't delay gratification, or twenty-year-olds who prefer to share everything with you rather than taking the risk needed to make intimate friends outside of the home. Children are supposed to achieve certain developmental milestones, and there are

plenty of good books and theories out there that explore this
idea. We like Erik Erikson's theory because it provides a
pretty clear "general map." Generally speaking, a five-year-
old should be able to tie his shoes, pick up her toys at the
end of the day, and wait a few minutes for something he
wants rather than going berserk unless immediate gratification occurs. A twenty-one-year-old should be able to reconcile a checkbook, pay bills without bouncing checks, have a
friendship network that replaces a good deal of the functions of his family of origin, and be able to hold down a job.

The more we do these things *for* our children at these
various ages, the more we infantilize them. And certainly,
the more confused and helpless we feel when contemplating
our children's lives, the more likely we are to have problems
in this area.

Letting Kids Run the Show

This overlaps somewhat with infantilizing. How do we
know when our kids are running the show? We know they
are when it feels like the adults aren't in charge. When there
are constant, miserable power struggles between parents
and children, and between parent and parent. When
children "divide and conquer" as in, "Mom said we can't go
out until we've finished our math homework. But can we go
out now and do it later?" When kids have become consummate negotiators, when parents have become consummate
nags, and when the tension in the house is so thick that
everyone feels stressed. We know our kids are running the
show when deep in our hearts we are beginning to resent
our children. That's how we know.

Specifically, our kids are running the show when they have five different toothbrushes from which to choose because you thought it would end the power struggle over brushing teeth, and it hasn't. He is running the show when you ask him to take out the garbage six times and then finally do it yourself, week after week, rather than finding a way to consistently enforce his doing this simple chore. Your daughter says she hates you after you tell her you can't afford to buy her a car. Because you can't tolerate her anger towards you, you cave into this transparent manipulation and buy her a car and pay the insurance on it in full, going further into debt, which creates ever more sleepless nights for you.

Do your children have horrendously foul mouths despite your repeated requests for them not to say the "f-word," the "s-word," and every other obscenity you've heard, and then some? When you ask them not to swear, do they just snicker and call you a name? Does it make your heart sink and your gut fill with rage at the same time when this happens? Or do your kids fight like barbarians all the time, shattering what little fragments of peace remain in your household, causing your blood pressure to remain elevated despite the new medication your doctor put you on? If these things are part of life in your household, then you have a problem.

Fix the Problem

Many of you already know how to fix the problem. In some families, the trouble isn't knowing how to fix these problems. It's recognizing that not fixing these problems will result in far more pain and suffering in the long run. There is no time like the present to begin helping kids grow up. Again, remember that one change instituted consistently can turn a whole system around. And don't try to change everything at once.

Infantilizing Kids

Below you will find a list of suggestions. Remember, life is not a test, it's an experiment, so being imperfect will not result in penalties in the game of life. So take a risk and try these suggestions. You will probably be pleasantly surprised by your results.

1. **Let 'em tie their own shoes!** Teach your five-year-old to tie her own shoes. Intentionally put an extra five or even ten minutes into your morning routine so that she will have time to tie her shoes herself. The first few times she gets it even approximately correct, notice and affirm her accomplishment. The incredible personal joy of accomplishing this task will sustain the behavior once it's learned.

2. **They won't break if they have to wait a few minutes.** When your eighteen-month-old awakens from his nap right when you're in the middle of turning those steaks or removing that soufflé from the oven, yell in a cheery voice that you'll be in to get him in just a minute. If he starts fussing, even if it's a really big fuss, continue doing what you're doing (unless it's going to take more than five or ten minutes). Then when you're done, walk confidently and cheerily into his room, thank him for waiting, and tend to his needs.

Don't make a big deal about it. Be as matter-of-fact as you can be. Exposing your children to very small doses of frustration like this will help them learn that waiting isn't the end of the world, and that they are separate from you. If you feel too guilty, know that it is a loving thing to help your child learn life's lessons.

3. **Let her tears do the healing.** When your fourteen-year-old daughter comes home from school in tears because her first boyfriend has apparently broken up with her (an event, by the way, that could be reversed tomorrow and then repeated the next day, given their ages), just listen. Be a good listener. Say things like, "It sounds like this is really painful for you. I'm sorry you hurt so much right now." Avoid giving her advice. Just listen, listen and listen some more.

   Sadness helps us heal. Tears come with sadness. Simply being with her sends a very powerful unconscious message that you believe she can handle life's pain. And of course, listening and validating are all that's needed to let her know that you care deeply for her.

4. **Don't bail him out!** Your twenty-one-year-old son, a senior in college, walks into the house after working at his fairly lucrative summer job and announces that he has somehow amassed a credit-card debt of $750 which he is unable to pay. Say, "Gee, that's a lot of money." Say this neutrally and with reverence. Do not smirk, do not look horrified, do not wring your hands, do not go into fix-it mode immediately. Wait a few moments. The pregnant pause will be uncomfortable for both of you, but when he realizes you aren't going

to bail him out, his mind will start to think about what has to be done. If he asks for you to pay it, very calmly say that you'd like to, but are much more afraid of what will happen if you do pay it off than if you don't. Then immediately ask, "Would you like some help figuring out how to juggle your finances and how to set up a budget and payment plan so you can get this paid off in a couple of summers?"

All parents would like to completely smooth the way for their children. It's only natural. Competent parents resist those urges because they know that over time, smoothing out all of life's rough edges will cripple their children and keep them from ever growing up. That's essentially the choice.

Letting Kids Run the Show

If you really want to do something about this and feel you need a pretty dramatic incentive, call the toll-free number and order that *20/20* segment about kids tyrannically running their households (see references at the end of this book). We doubt anyone could watch that program and not be stirred to action by what they see.

4

Put Your
Marriage Last

When a couple first comes in for relationship therapy, a question we ask is: "How long has it been since the two of you got away by yourselves, without the kids, for an overnight stay?" We found that this can be a helpful question. It is good for the couple and the children to experience this balance in a family, with ease and security. In this country, it appears to be quite common for parents to go one year, two, three, five, sometimes even more years, without getting away overnight without their children. Of course, new parents can experience some struggle or guilt, but if their children are being well cared for, we support and encourage this stretch for parents and children. When a strong marital relationship is visible to the children, we see children relax and thrive.

Are You a PCU?

We Americans pride ourselves on how outgoing, moral and family-oriented we are. Next to the Irish, from whom we have inherited many of our child-rearing practices and attitudes, we are perhaps the most child-centered of the western industrialized nations. Believe it or not, this can be a problem because a marriage or other long-term relationship is a living, breathing organism that is continually renewing itself, repairing its wounds, growing and changing. As such, it needs to be nurtured and cared for or it will wither and die. It needs to be watered. It needs to be weeded and pruned. It needs sunlight. It needs time to rest and recuperate. A relationship that is externally focused to the exclusion of itself will surely wilt.

Remember that the opposite of dysfunction is dysfunction. It is equally unhealthy for parents to neglect their children, to leave the kids with a sitter, overnight, *all* the time. Obviously, disturbed parents, like those we occasionally read about in the newspaper, who leave their little ones home alone while they fly off on vacation for several days are guilty of child neglect and abandonment. However, this chapter is targeted directly to those many American parents who are so overly attached to their kids, or who are still suffering from so many ghosts of their own pasts, that they can't separate from their children even long enough to take care of their marriages now and then. If you don't know who you are, you can know by looking to see if your marriage is wilting.

For over a decade, we have kept a tattered clipping of an Ann Landers column that reported on a nice piece of research conducted at the National Institute of Mental Health. In this study, the investigators located fifty parents who had successfully raised their children into healthy adulthood. They simply asked these parents to offer suggestions and pointers about how to raise healthy children. As you might expect, these competent parents mentioned things like "listening to your child," saying "please" and "thank you," and "not expecting to be perfect parents." As you may have guessed by now, after mentioning "the importance of loving your child and making her feel like she belongs," they listed *"make the needs of your mate a priority— child-centered families make neither healthy parents nor healthy children."*

Did you ever wonder why so many empty-nest divorces occur? Often, on the surface at least, you may see a perfect couple with perfect children who live in a perfect family. They may do lots of family things together, and it may seem that they are warm and loving and cooperative and successful, and then their kids grow up. So, why a divorce now?

Flip back a page or so, and you'll know. In many of the empty-nest divorces that we have witnessed, the truth is that the couple has not really been connecting as a couple for decades. They have simply been functioning as what we have termed a *Parental Childrearing Unit,* or a PCU. A PCU is a style of relationship in which the partners have, for numerous reasons, made an implicit, unconscious bargain to over-focus on their children and under-focus on their marriages. It is sometimes done because that is how each of the partners was raised, and other times it is done in the hopes that if they try really hard with their own kids, they will be able to make up for some perceived lack or pain in their own childhoods.

What about when the kids are really young? Don't they require more than the marriage in many cases? Of course. This is a gradual process. But children aren't young forever. And even parents of overly active infants find ways to take time to nurture their marriages. There are many ways to tend to your marital garden.

For example, we believe it makes sense for children to sleep in their own beds. How in the world can a couple, already stretched to the limits by kids, television, traffic, two jobs, noise, pollution and computers, expect to find any time to nurture their relationship? How about for those few minutes each night as they wearily but warmly whisper to each other in the comfortably dimmed privacy of their own bed as they prepare to fall asleep so they can face another hectic day tomorrow? You can't if you have a child in your bed all the time.

Even if you are the parent of very young children, you can still take time to take care of your marriage. Honest. You can. People who are ecstatic at the prospect of their empty nest (once they grieve the leaving of their last child) have managed to do it. The people in that National Institute of Mental Health study did it. You can do it, too.

Where's the Passion?

Ah, passion. And chemistry. And magic. We all know that they are supposed to leave a marriage after a few years to be replaced by those old saws—companionship, comfort and friendship. Companionship, comfort and friendship are essential elements in a wonderful marriage. But so are passion, chemistry, magic and sexuality. In her wonderful research-based book on healthy marriages, psychologist Catherine Johnson wrote that most happy marriages are held together by a "powerful and enduring" sexual bond— even when partners are not fully aware of it. So, what do you make of that?

Most of what we learn while we are growing up is below the conscious level. We just pick it up by being immersed in the family. This means that we all learn the lessons of our own particular families. Perhaps Mother always made your school lunches for you, and Father always gave you extra spending money "on the side." If so, these things would just seem normal to us. That is how our lessons are learned. Sometimes we all need to learn additional lessons. For example, some people will need to learn how to nurture their marriages, while others will have learned this all through childhood by simply being in the family and being around Mom and Dad's marriage.

Most family systems therapists know that sexuality and passion are woven throughout the fabric of the family. St. Paul psychologists James Maddock and Noel Larson wrote that "sexuality is a fundamental aspect of human existence. It is one of [the] basic dimensions of human experience, and

thus of family life" (p. 51). Sexuality isn't just about repro-
duction. Passion isn't just about intercourse. They both
relate to an underlying energy that pervades the family, or
else a lack of that underlying energy. This does not mean
that loud, boisterous people are filled with healthy passion,
or that quiet people are not. It has nothing to do with intro-
version or extroversion or with boisterousness or quietness.
It has to do with energy. There are as many calm, reflective
people who are filled with passion and a lust for life as there
are loud people who are not, and vice versa. It has to do with
energy, passion, focus, expansion, determination, life-force
and a desire to live life fully. A passion for life is woven into
the substrate of healthy families that is missing or deficient
in troubled families.

This passion may appear as a desire to express ourselves
through our art or music, through our parenting, or through
our scientific explorations. It is our confidence about ourselves, and our passion for life, that underlies and fuels our
sexuality. When people are depressed, burned out, overworked, frightened of each other or of their own feelings,
then it is difficult to experience healthy, balanced, open sexuality. When we feel competent, relaxed and open to the
mysteries of life, then our sexuality is comfortable, passionate and balanced.

You might ask, "But what happens to a couple if the kids
don't want to go to bed at their regular bedtime?" If you are
nurturing your marriage and also providing structure for
your children, then the kids will have a regular bedtime
because you know that this is good for them and for you.
They won't fuss and scream and pout and posture. They will

simply go to bed. If they don't, then just keep your bedroom door locked. They will figure out that Dad and Mom have their own life in addition to their life with their children. Are there exceptions, such as when a small child is sick? Of course.

Parents: The Executives in the System

All of the unconscious rules for living and interacting in a family flow from the executives in the system—from the parents. If there is only one parent in the family because of death or total abandonment, then all the rules flow from that one parent and any other adults who are regularly in his or her life. If you grew up ashamed of your tears, you learned that somewhere. If you grew up defensive, angry and confrontational, you learned that somewhere. If you grew up seeing that the children always come first, then you will need to stay mindful to keep your marriage from becoming one of parental childrearing units. Because the parents in the family system are always instructing the children on the rules about how to live and interact with each other, the family, and the outside world, we support our clients to explore and become familiar with all the rules they have learned. We especially support them in keeping at least a small part of their lives to themselves.

Signs in You That You Don't Have a Marital Life

If you have strayed into this trap, here are some of the things to look for. When you are least prepared to do it, stop right in the middle of your busy day and take five minutes to quietly, silently reflect on the status of your inner life and on the status of your marriage/partnership. Do you feel satisfied? Whole? Competent? Emotionally present every once in awhile? When you think about your relationship, what do you hear from the depths of your unconscious? Does that voice say, "It's time for you and her to plan another mini-vacation, before your relationship starts to wilt"? Or does it say, "I think we need to go to a movie by ourselves tonight"? Maybe it says, "Let's turn off the television set tonight and just chatter away about our day." Remember, too, that one of the best all-around barometers for the health of a relationship is the quality of your sex life.

You know you're in trouble when there is no place the two of you can go where there isn't a child present. There are kids in your bed, kids in your bathroom, kids in your den or office, kids in your car. There are always kids on your vacations. They are always with you when you go out to dinner. They are always there. The key word here is: "always." A healthier phrase might be, "much or even most of the time." Good parents spend a lot of time with their kids. They also spend enough time alone, with each other, with no kids in sight, to keep their marriages going.

Signs in Your Children That You Don't Have a Marital Life

Kids who have been raised by PCUs have certain common features that are often evident. They are sometimes, but not always, pretty dependent on you. It is not the whiny, helpless, victimy kind of dependency. Rather, it is the kind of kid who has a hard time going away to college, or into the world, or who chooses to stay at home or stay too close to home when other options are there. He might say he's staying close to home "Because I really love my family and want to be near them." It's the kid who calls you her best friend and who spends an inordinate amount of time with you when she ought to be out in the world making friends and finding a mate of her own.

Sometimes it shows up with confused boundaries, like when you're there, they're there. Your stuff is their stuff. When they're a little older, they are often privy to the details of your lives that should be reserved for you. They know about your finances. They know about your hopes, dreams, fears and regrets (some of which is okay). In some families, they even know about your sex life! They seem to be experts on the inner workings of your marriage.

When PCU-raised kids enter adulthood, they sometimes do it half-heartedly. When they enter into a long-term committed relationship, they sometimes do it half-heartedly. Sometimes their family-of-origin remains more important to them than their mate, which causes obvious problems. And if their parents' marriage should falter, many of these adult children can find themselves shattered or in the middle of their parents' mess, or both.

How to Fix It

What do you do if you suspect that you may have a problem in this area of your life? If you are identifying this as a problem, then you have already begun. Then take a good look at your relationship—your strengths and weaknesses, fears, hopes, and dreams. Talk to each other from the heart. Forget the invisible rules that say, "You are not a nice person if you share your real feelings with your spouse," or "If you talk about these difficult things, it will ruin your marriage." Let the tears of relief flow along with the hurt, anger, loneliness, fear and joy. Renowned sex therapist and psychologist David Schnarch wrote that intimacy "involves the inherent awareness that you're separate from your partner, with parts yet to be shared" (p. 102). In other words, sharing the nitty-gritty stuff, even if it's uncomfortable, can deepen your intimacy beyond measure.

Ask yourselves when you last got away by yourselves without the kids. Tell each other how much you resent the kids being in your bedroom all the time, and how you've been obsessing about telling your partner about this for years but were afraid of the reaction. Discuss any intense guilt you both feel at the thought of cutting back just a little bit on how involved your kids are in your lives, or any feelings you harbor that you've been hurting your kids. Talk about it. Entertain the faint possibility that what you are reading right now may be correct, and that the way you have been doing it all these years has been an unconscious habit. It is worth changing, for everyone.

Next, sit down and figure out how and when you will make time for your marriage. Some of our suggestions include:

1. Taking a small bit of time each day, if only for a few minutes, to really talk
2. Setting aside at least an evening per week for a date
3. At a bare minimum, taking one vacation each year that does not include the kids
4. Find competent, quality baby-sitters for children of various ages

If money is an issue, remember that you don't have to fly first-class to Hawaii and stay in an oceanfront room at the Mauna Kea Beach Hotel on The Big Island to get away by yourselves. Camping one night at the nearest campground counts just as much. If your children are infants or toddlers, ask yourselves why they haven't experienced a babysitter yet. Assuming that the babysitter provides quality care, and is good rather than abusive—which is still very possible to find—know that it is an important, healthy separation experience for your kids to see you leave, cry as you drive away, have a great time with the sitter and then awaken the next morning to discover that the two of you are happily home. When children are robbed of healthy separation experiences today, they often have separation anxiety and lack the ability to form trusting relationships as adults.

Of course, you must make sure that the kids have a regular bedtime that is consistently enforced. If the kids are older, then they must be quiet after a certain time—no television blaring in the family room at all hours of the night, no telephones ringing or friends coming and going long after you've gone to bed. Invest in a lock for your bedroom door. Install the lock on your bedroom door. Use the lock on your bedroom door. When is the last time you felt like making love when, at any moment, a child could burst through the door to ask you where his underwear is, or where she left her jewelry case or to get a glass of water, or to just see what you're up to? If it's hard enough to maintain romance when our children are young, it's nearly impossible to do so without locks on doors. Again, there are exceptions, like when you have a very sick child.

And So?

Remember that the goal is not to swing from one extreme to the other. We do not condone child neglect and abandonment, no matter what the justification. Our children need us to show up at their band concerts, hockey games, school plays and church choir concerts. They need us to chauffeur them to the doctor and the dentist. They need us to create a sense of family and belonging, of togetherness, of unity. They need to see what a healthy marriage looks like, how it functions, how problems are dealt with and how conflicts are negotiated.

Children also need to see that Dad and Mom have magic and chemistry between them. No, they do not need to see Dad and Mom sexually mauling each other in the kitchen when Mom gets home from work. This would be a form of sexual abuse, actually. But to see a hint of what's there—a sparkle in Mom's eye, a twinkle in Dad's, a pat on the back, a look, a glance, a kiss that's just a little longer than the usual kind that relatives get, and those date nights when Dad and Mom get dressed up and go out on the town without the kids—these are the basis of the enchanted, unconscious, romantic images burned into a child's brain that allow the future adult to value magic and chemistry. They need to see an exclusivity in their parents' marriage, beyond which no children are able to pass. They need to see Dad and Mom having a life.

5

Push Your Child into Too Many Activities

More! More! More!

Somewhere on the way to the twenty-first century, it seems as if the majority of middle-class parents decided that it would be a good thing to work themselves to death—and then just for good measure, they decided to work their children to death, too. For many years, the most common sexual dysfunction in Americans hasn't been impotence or the inability to have an orgasm. The most common one is lack of desire. You may be asking yourself, "What does that have to do with raising kids?" But indirectly, it does. Lack of desire comes from a couple of places, one being the sad fact that many adults are overextended and worked to death. The other, related to the first, is that sexual desire and sexual intimacy typically occur in the context of emotional intimacy. But it's hard to have emotional intimacy when your life is spinning out of control.

In a December 1997 article in the Minneapolis *StarTribune*, Steve Berg wrote that the new *simplicity movement* "doesn't imply dropping out or going cheapskate. Rather, it suggests a more balanced approach to life and a realization that Americans are both beneficiaries and victims of an economy fed by the relentless drive to consume— a condition that simplifiers sometimes call 'affluenza.'" *Both beneficiary and victim.* There's the rub. It's not all bad, but it surely isn't all good. As practicing psychologists, we are acutely aware of the negative impact of affluenza on our clients. Families become so outer-directed, so focused on producing, earning, spending and then earning some more to keep up with the next round of spending that there is hardly any time left for anything else. "Anything else" means: family, joy, laughter, feelings, sex, play, dreaming and grieving, among others.

To give you a startling example of what we mean here, let's look at the beginning of each of our therapy sessions with clients. In our therapy rooms, at client's-eye-view, we have a list of the basic emotions that human beings experience. They are all good, healthy emotions. They are: anger, sadness, joy, hurt, shame, fear, guilt and loneliness. At the beginning of each session, we do what is called a "feelings check," which is simply a chance for each client in the room to reflect inside and notice what he or she is feeling. This helps the person get grounded in the moment and pay attention to his or her own inner goings-on. It sounds easy enough, but it is actually one of the more difficult things we ask our clients to do, and over the past decade it has become increasingly difficult for people. People are so focused on deadlines, goals, schedules, meetings, phones, faxes and production that many are now stuck in a near-permanent state of dissociation from their feelings. "Dissociation" is just another way of saying disconnection, separation or being oblivious. It has become so bad in some cases that the only responses a client can muster are "confused," "numb," "nothing," "I feel fine," or the extremely frequent, "I don't know."

If it sounds like a trivial exercise, ask yourself how you could possibly have anything more than a very superficial emotional relationship with someone if you can't access each and every emotion on our list. And if you can convince us, we'll give you our house and both automobiles, no questions asked. Remember, though, we said "emotional relationship." You know, like a marriage or long-term love relationship, a deep friendship, or a parent-child relationship. See? It's a trick offer. You can't have an emotional relationship without access to your emotions. It would be a metaphysical impossibility. But more importantly, millions of Americans lose every day by being so driven that even if they had learned to express emotions as children, they wouldn't have the time or wherewithal to do so now. No emotions means no emotional intimacy. No time for emotions means no time for emotional intimacy. No time for emotional intimacy? Then forget having an emotionally connected family. And *definitely* forget having a warm, ful-filling, wonderful sex life.

Excellent Grades, Not-So-Excellent Life

So, what *has* happened to the American family on the way to the twenty-first century? Too much, too fast? Excess? And not just materially. Too many activities. During the question-and-answer period of a professional seminar we were presenting, a very bright psychologist raised her hand and said, "But what about all the advice the colleges and high schools are giving us—that our kids won't get into the best universities unless they have umpteen million extracurricular activities on their resumes?" Good question. Two-part answer. A Duke University senior told us, "The universities are looking for depth. Two outside accomplishments done with depth will go as far, if not farther, than umpteen million scattered activities that were obviously done to beef up one's application." Duke is currently ranked as one of the top three universities in the nation, according to *U.S. News and World Report.*

Second, over the years, our caseload has been filled with young professionals whose parents anxiously pressed them harder and harder to excel and achieve during high school and college out of an imaginary fear that "If my child doesn't go to the best and become the best, his or her life will be miserable." Well, they are miserable, all right, not for want of being the best, but because of trying to be to the exclusion of everything else that is more important in life. In *Emotional*

Intelligence: Why It Can Matter More Than IQ, Daniel Goleman wrote about some remarkable studies conducted at Harvard in the 1940s and in Illinois high schools in the early 1980s.

In the Harvard study, men with the highest grades were found to be less happy, less adjusted, less productive and to have lower salaries and status in middle age than their college peers who had lower grades in college. Of eighty-one high school valedictorians in Illinois, only a fourth "were at the highest level of young people of comparable age in their chosen profession" ten years later, "and many were doing much less well." Goleman quoted Karen Arnold, professor of education at Boston University: "To know that a person is a valedictorian is to know only that he or she is exceedingly good at achievement as measured by grades. *It tells you nothing about how they react to the vicissitudes of life*" (p. 35; emphasis added). This is our answer to the woman who wanted to know about kids' activities and college. *You can push your kids until they drop, and then push them a lot more, but the only thing you will produce are miserable adults who* may *become moderately successful in their careers, if they are lucky.*

The child may be father to the man, but the parents determine how the child fares. Driven parents produce: (1) children who are themselves driven to fill in the void left by being emotionally neglected, or (2) children who don't care about succeeding much at all because they're so lonely, hurt and angry about being neglected. Remember that the opposite of unhealthy is unhealthy.

What to Do Instead

1. Ask Yourself If Your Child Is Balanced

Remember the extremes. If you are one of those parents who does not expect much from your children, then this chapter does not apply to you. Competence, and therefore high self-esteem, come from struggle and effort, not from mollycoddling. But if your children are in a hurricane of activity from early in the morning until late at night, then try using the following simple yardstick: *If your child can get As, do three activities well, is not getting sick regularly (this includes emotional illnesses such as depression, addictions and getting stuck in destructive relationships), still has time for a social life as well as family time, and is able to maintain access to his or her emotions, then your child is probably doing just fine.*

On the other hand, if your child is getting sick regularly, has no social life or social skills, has no time whatsoever to be with the family, is numb or blunted emotionally—if any one of these is present for your child—then it is clearly time for a change. Maybe Bs or Cs are realistic goals. Maybe a state university, a community college or a vocational-technical school is where your child belongs. For the sake of your own peace of mind, ask yourself if you can think of any great leaders, business people, successful inventors or entrepreneurs who didn't even graduate from college. If you can't think of any, then go to the library or get on the Internet or talk to your neighbors or colleagues or friends at church or your child's teachers or *somebody*. Or read Goleman's *Emotional Intelligence*. You will discover that there is much more to success, to life and to happiness than getting straight As in school or going to an Ivy League university.

2. Examine Your Own Values

It is gratifying to watch adults struggle with what is important to them. As many of you have already learned, life keeps tossing the same lesson in front of us until we learn it, and then we get to move on to the next lesson. If the primary lesson we need to learn right now is about how we spend our time and energy, then life will put it right in our faces, over and over, until we learn it. Many Americans are struggling with this right now. It's about values. It's about what's important to us. And what's important to us becomes very clear to our children whether we tell them or not. They learn it in how we live our lives.

We all need to strike a balance. We must ask ourselves if it is part of our values to say, "You are very important to us. It's just that right now we have to produce as much as we can because we want to get that new boat for summer." This is what Gregory Bateson called a double-bind—damned if you do, damned if you don't. Your children can't say, "We don't want a boat; we want time with you," because of the look on your face, and because of how much you've talked about getting a new boat. You've talked about it so much, in fact, that your children aren't even aware that it's the extra hours of work to pay for the boat that's numbing your relationship with them. Your children have been seduced into believing, like you, that a new boat will bring the intimacy for which they long. But it won't, at least not if you have to work yourself to death to get it. So, a part of your child says, "I hate this boat idea," and another part says, "This boat will save our family." It's an insidious trap.

Many people have confused love with working too hard for too many material things, thinking that these things are so essential to their well-being that they begin to literally live for their things. All you have to do is ask yourself, "If someone else were trying to determine what my values were by following me around during a typical week, what would they discover?" Ask yourself this question, and for your sake and for the sake of your family, let yourself hear the answer.

3. First, Make Adjustments to Yourself

Perhaps the most elusive bit of wisdom that we must all eventually acquire if we want to be competent people and parents is the fact that the only effective way to change things in anyone's life is to change yourself. You can't make someone else change.

What we do as parents matters. We choose the family road. You can try to force your children to be polite or successful or truthful or to take calculated risks, but if you don't do these things yourself, you will swim against a current that will overpower you. You can lead them in a certain direction or you can convince them to change themselves, but you can't make them change in any enduring way unless it makes sense to them. What makes sense to children is what they see going on around them. Whatever you do will be what they do, whatever you believe is what they will believe, whatever you value is what they'll value. Yes, they might do the exact opposite, also.

Some people are driven to work excessively because of *affluenza*. If too many resource-draining possessions are driving your excessive working, then one way to restore intimacy and balance in your family life might be to get rid of some of your stuff. When you and your spouse sell your $300,000 house and buy a $175,000 one (home prices vary from one part of the country to the next, of course) so that you won't have to work so hard to make ends meet, you will send one of the most powerful messages you can send to your children. Will they grumble and whine and get stressed out by the change? Probably. They'll no doubt go through a miniature version of what you experience—feeling ashamed about the downsizing at first, worrying what others will think, grieving the loss of some of the conveniences that came with the more expensive house. But if you and your partner steadfastly follow through with the decision and remain reverent about it while doing it, then everyone will be just fine. In fact, everyone will be better off than they ever imagined possible. And in the end, you will have displayed an unparalleled act of courage, commitment to values and follow-through that will be stored in your children's memory banks for the rest of their lives. What greater gift could a parent give to a child?

4. Discuss with Your Children the Possibility of Cutting Back on Activities—If That Doesn't Work, Intervene

This is pretty straightforward. If you have been display-ing occasional examples of courageous changes in your own lifestyle for awhile, then it will not appear or feel uncon-sciously hypocritical to your children when you sit down with them and have a face-to-face, heart-to-heart talk about their being overextended. Sometimes children and teenagers shed tears of relief when someone steps in and says, "We want to talk to you about how much you have to do every week. It feels like too much, and we're concerned about you." When you make a direct statement like this, with the primary message being that you care, it goes right around a person's defenses and wraps itself around their heart. The person who receives such a powerful message will melt.

You might find it comforting to know that in our expe-rience, many of the people who have serious problems such as alcoholism or depression are actually relieved when we ask directly, "Do you think you have a drinking problem?" or say and ask directly, "You know, I think you've been struggling with depression for a long time. Were you aware of that?" Diane Naas, a friend of ours who does chemical dependency interventions with professionals, once told the story of the quickest intervention she ever encountered. After several weeks of preparation with concerned family members and friends, during which they role-played what to say, how to say it, where to sit and how to get this powerful man to the intervention in the first place, the day of reckoning arrived. Everyone assembled in the large executive boardroom and readied themselves. They were so nervous they could barely breathe. The man's boss—the CEO of the corporation—escorted him to the boardroom under the pretense that they were having an emergency meeting to handle a work-related crisis. The man walked into the room, looked around at the anxious, loving, caring, frightened and very determined faces in the room and said, simply, "Okay. I'm ready. Where do you want me to go to treatment?"

As psychologists, one of the more wonderful aspects of our job is to see this sort of thing happen. At some level, most of us know what's best for us even if we aren't ready to do it. It is remarkable how many of us are just waiting for someone who cares about us to put it into words: "I see you're hurting," "I see you drink a lot," "I'm concerned about how little sleep you're getting," or "We want to talk to you about how much you have to do every week. It feels like too much, and we're concerned about you." You can talk about things this directly with those whom you love, and it will change your life and theirs.

5. Follow Through, Follow Through, Then Follow Through Some More

The difference between one who is successful and one who is not is the ability to follow through with something after the first glow of new insight has worn off. Follow-through is what takes place after all has been said and before anything has been done. Follow-through is the real stuff of life. It is the integrity to keep putting one foot in front of the other even when we'd rather stop.

So when it comes to your kids being stretched to the limit and wrung out, you have to acknowledge the problem and then follow through. First, turn off the television. The television is one thing that keeps you from following through with anything else. Second, spend some time alone with yourself. If you spend some time truly alone with yourself, as opposed to time alone with yourself along with the radio, television, dog, newspaper and neighbor-over-the-fence, you will hear things that will help you follow through. Third, know that it will hurt, and then it will hurt some more, and then just when you thought the hurt would end, it will hurt some more. It will get a lot better, too. Day after day after day, it will get better. And then just when you thought it would always be better, it will get worse. At this point, your commitment to follow-through will be more important than anyone could ever imagine.

And then one day it will get better and stay better, because it will have become a *habit*. You and your children now have lives again. You and they aren't sick and tired all the time. You aren't as driven. The five of you actually sit down together for dinner a few nights a week, where you converse comfortably and warmly, knowing that one of you doesn't have to rush off to yet another meeting or practice. You gaze around at the smaller house that is almost paid for and breathe a sigh of relief, grateful that you got off the treadmill that was draining the spirit right out of you. You look in your appointment book and realize that there *is* time for a vacation, or a weekend away now and then. You look at your children and notice, peacefully, that they are beginning to know who they are and where they want to go with their lives. They look healthier. Everyone acts healthier. Everyone *is* healthier. Congratulations.

6

Ignore Your Emotional or Spiritual Life

As we neared the completion of this manuscript, Dean Ornish released his new book *Love and Survival*, which focuses on the emotional/spiritual aspects of his ground-breaking program to reverse coronary artery disease. It is difficult to express how pleased and relieved we were when word of Ornish's program first spread throughout the professional community several years ago. As he points out in his newest book, a large number of excellent research studies link the quality of your relationships with your physical health. But it is Ornish, a respected physician at the University of California San Francisco Medical Center—a highly regarded, traditional medical establishment—who is now stating publicly, and with solid research support to back him up, that *love makes a big difference to our physical health*. While this may not startle you, keep in mind that it borders on the bizarre in the estimation of many otherwise rational physicians and scientists. Ornish notes that in an exhaustive search of the medical literature, he could find only two articles out of nine million that included both the words "love" and "heart disease."

Up to the Mountaintop, and into the Muddle

Spirituality is such a broad concept, with so many meanings, that it confuses many of us at one time or another. While it may be trite to do so, we will point out that spirituality and religion are not the same thing, even though they may be highly related at times. We tend toward viewing spirituality as a capacity inherent in all human beings, like the capacity to grow, reproduce, communicate, think or feel. Of course, some hard-nosed scientists would disagree with that last statement.

If you can accept that spirituality is a capacity inherent in all human beings, then the next question is, "A capacity for what?" For transcendence? For existing in a nonphysical plane? For communicating with others across thousands of miles or even light years without the aid of physical devices? The list is so long that we prefer to narrow it down a bit. We like to think of spirituality as (1) the capacity to have a relationship with something beyond ourselves, which for some is a personal God and for others is $e = mc^2$; (2) a feeling that often includes a deep sense of connection with all of creation; and (3) a sense of awe and wonder about the universe that is impossible to describe. You most likely experienced this third aspect of spirituality the last time you stared deeply into the night sky and realized that you were both infinitesimally, insignificantly puny and at one with the universe in the same instant.

Spirituality is closely related to sexuality, humility, shame, gratitude, love and power, among other things. Spiritual people have wisdom, which translates into knowing when to try to change things and when not to, when to surrender and when to struggle some more, when to fight city hall and when not to fight city hall. Whether they are celibate or not, spiritual people embrace and celebrate their sexuality as the way in which each of us is connected to all of creation—it is our life force, our energy and our passion for life. Because the function of healthy shame is to let us be accountable and therefore transcend our own human limita tions, spirituality is closely tied to shame, which in turn is closely tied to humility and gratitude, which are capacities necessary for us to be truly powerful.

If you look at most of the world's religions, you'll probably notice that spirituality is expressed, experienced or practiced in two ways. One is to go to the proverbial mountaintop and pray; the other, which is very earthy indeed, is to muck about amidst the din and confusion and messiness of humanity. The first one is easy for most people to understand. We are alone with our thoughts, and we look skyward and briefly converse with God. We ask God to help us get through a difficult time, or to look after a friend who is in trouble. People who do this, including the 20 percent of atheists and agnostics who regularly pray (according to research by sociologist Father Andrew Greeley), are certainly expressing their spirituality.

But the other aspect of expressing spirituality has historically given us human beings a run for our money. We are taught that our daily labor has dignity and value, and is an expression of our spirituality—whether it be washing dishes, programming computers, doing open-heart surgery or ministering to the sick and dying in the streets of Calcutta. Most of us understand the reasoning behind such a statement. We "get it." But do we really "get it"? Do we really feel it and breathe it into our souls every day? Do we really understand why the book is titled *Chop Wood, Carry Water* (because it emphasizes the importance of ordinary tasks in being a spiritual person), or why, in *The Karate Kid*, Mr. Miyagi began training his pupil by having him wax his car, saying to Daniel, "Wax on, wax off"? With an unemployment rate at its lowest in decades and with so many middle- and upper-middle-class kids being indulged with most everything they want, it is understandable that many children miss this spiritual connection and view work as demeaning and pointless. This distorted sense of entitlement makes being spiritual very hard.

Catholic anthropologist and mystic Teilhard de Chardin wrote, "The depths of matter are merely a reflection of the heights of spirit." What a lovely statement. But if you have been given more things than anyone could ever need in five lifetimes, then that statement becomes empty. Many addicts will tell you that one of their greatest fears and biggest impediments to recovery is the fear of life becoming boring.

When you translate this in light of the discussion above, what it really means is that many *unrecovering* addicts have a hard time detecting or appreciating subtleties and nuances. It takes a great deal of depth to be able to appreciate the little daily things of life.

Dignity, wisdom, grace and power all flow from our connection to and relationship with the daily details of living. Yes, it is difficult to remain spiritually centered after your house has been destroyed by a flood, earthquake or tornado. But it is also hard to remain spiritually centered when you are stalled in traffic on a smoggy, sticky, hot summer day; or when you have a headache, your neck is sore, your back is aching and you still have five more shirts to iron, or twenty more pages to study, or three more errands to do, and all you want to do is go home.

How to Sabotage Spirituality in Eleven Easy Lessons

Okay. You can go to the mountaintop and pray, or you can hang around with other humans and try to love each other, and while you're doing that, you can all try to care for the planet and the creatures on it. That's spirituality. But as we also noted above, many of us seem to be so rushed and so frantic to produce more and do it faster, that true spirituality is as remote as the outer reaches of the universe. So, here are some of the common blocks to spirituality that we see parents promoting or embracing.

1. Humility Isn't Cool (Arrogance)

We're not sure when this attitude began, but when parents are embarrassed to admit that they believe in God or that science doesn't necessarily have all the answers, then children learn that it "isn't cool" to believe such things. When parents would like to go to a religious service but are afraid of what their intellectual friends might think, then of course, children learn the same thing. Even more, when parents are too embarrassed to admit their embarrassment, then children learn that humility and gratitude are for the weak, rather than for the powerful.

2. You Can't Trust Anyone These Days (Cynicism)

The world has become more complex and more compressed than ever before. People from tribes who once hated each other find themselves working side-by-side at airline ticket counters, in hospitals and on construction sites. Old enemies and threats are replaced by new ones, as evidenced by our fear of terrorists using chemical and biological weapons. In the United States, gun ownership has reached such tragic proportions that it is truly healthy, normal behavior to feel waves of fear sweep over you if you inadvertently offend another driver on the freeway. And for goodness' sake, don't ever park your car in a suburban shopping mall without first scanning all around you to see if a carjacker is lurking behind another vehicle, just waiting to stick a gun in your face.

It may be partly true that "People are no damned good,"

but it is also true that many people are *very good*. John Steinbeck captured the magic of human goodness in his opening description of the colorful human beings who lived in Monterey's *Cannery Row*:

> *Its inhabitants are, as the man once said, whores, pimps, gamblers, and sons of bitches, by which he meant everybody. Had the man looked through another peephole he might have said saints and angels and martyrs and holy men and he would have meant the same thing.*

People are basically pretty decent. Rich or poor, Catholic or Jew, male or female, when the chips are down we're all doing the best we can. Yes, at times people are no damned good, and if you choose to focus your energy there, that's what you'll see. But it is hard to be connected to others when you fear and hate them, which makes it hard to be spiritual.

3. There Isn't Enough Time (Fear or Greed)

If we are indeed the most hurried and harried bunch of human beings in planetary history, is it not because we are overworked, overstressed and just plain too busy? And are these things not a sign of being too greedy—I want more and the only way I'll get it is to work harder? Or a sign of being scared—if I stop busying myself to exhaustion I won't have enough to survive or to be happy? How can you go to the mountaintop and meditate when you don't have time to shave at home so you do it in the car on the way to work? Of course, there are other reasons that some people work too hard, including the single dad or mom who is just trying to make it. We're referring here to overwork that you believe is necessary, but isn't.

If we sincerely value our spiritual development, then we have to carve out just a little bit of time to be alone with ourselves and the universe. Now and then we give our clients an assignment to take time each day to be alone and still. When they return the next week, they often report what an eye-opening and meaningful experience it was. What makes it such a challenge for many is that it includes no radio, no television, no pets, no journal, no books, no friends, no video games, nothing—just uninterrupted, unimpeded, silent alone-time.

If you think you're just too busy to pray or meditate, remember that people pray all the time. You can be stuck in the middle of rush-hour traffic, leaning on your horn, fuming, focusing on the chaos, and in a split-second you can turn it all around by simply paying attention to your breathing as you say silently, "Thank you for this day." During stress-reduction training, busy people can shut their office doors for five minutes while they close their eyes and breathe through an entire relaxation protocol that leaves them refreshed and focused again, no matter how hectic the day has been or will be. In the middle of a delicate surgery, your doctor may think to herself, "God, help me do a good job today."

Parents who take time for prayer or meditation create households where others know that this is being done. In these homes, spirituality is being demonstrated, encouraged and supported. Children's behavior is astonishingly predictable once you have a fairly good sampling of parents' behavior. This goes for private behavior, too, such as praying. Parents who are sincerely humble, grateful and prayerful (as opposed to inauthentically so) produce children who are much the same.

4. I Must Be Happy Right Now—Struggle Is Bad (Impatience, Immaturity)

The capacity to value and enjoy struggle is such a definitive part of being a competent human being that, in our belief, people who do not value struggle will be trapped in infancy until they can learn to embrace it. There is so much confusion about this, too. How much struggle is enough? What if my children struggle too much? When does it become abuse? Isn't it good to remove as much struggle as possible? Wouldn't I be better off putting my energy elsewhere?

To struggle is to be alive. To be alive is to exert and express your being in the world. To express your being in the world is part of spirituality. The total absence of struggle only exists prior to conception and, depending upon your beliefs, after you die. Struggle contributes to the meaning and value of life. Removing all the struggle from your children's lives prevents their growth, and also prevents them from being alive. Children who have been chronically indulged are sometimes like zombies. They seem to lack spirit, energy and drive. Sometimes they are angry, scared, disappointed and demanding. And it's our responsibility if it happens. Our kids need us to let them learn to struggle. They deserve nothing less from us.

5. It's Every Man for Himself—I'd Rather Do It Myself (Narcissism, Isolation and Loneliness)

Erik Erikson suggested that America was built on a socio-cultural foundation that skipped his first stage of human development: trust versus mistrust. This may surprise you because many Americans pride themselves in how friendly they are, and in how quickly they rush to aid a neighbor in need. But intimacy has many levels. While you are helping your neighbor build a garage, you may be unaware that he is depressed or having marital problems. Have you ever been the one who has been continuously busy in the kitchen help-ing out the hostess because you secretly fear sustained social interaction with others? Do you have *any* relationships in which you share deeply with another about yourself? Would you be terribly shocked to discover that your seemingly blissful neighbors were terribly worried about their teenage son? It is very possible to have a great deal of interaction with friends and neighbors but have no idea of what is really going on in their lives. This is what Erikson meant, we suspect.

6. If You Can't See It and Measure It, It Isn't Real (Skepticism)

Here come the hard-nosed scientists again, bless their hearts. Skepticism can be a good thing, just like optimism is. Up to a point. And then skepticism starts to erode your spirituality. The ability to have awe and wonder about the universe, and the ability to appreciate the (as yet)

unknowable parts of the universe, are essential features of
spirituality. Perhaps we should say that unbending skepticism is harmful to your spirit. After all, Jesus loved his
doubting Thomas as much as the rest of his apostles, and
Thomas was one of the apostles for a reason.

Also remember that there is more than one way to "see."
Sometimes very poor decisions come from people who are
very intelligent in a rational way but who have little access
to their emotions, and who therefore decide things with
only half of the information available to them. Two people
observing the exact same human interaction may interpret
what is going on in very different ways. "Seeing" is not
always what it seems. Ask yourself how you can see with
your heart as well as with your head.

7. What Difference Can One Person Make? (Powerlessness)

When Mother Teresa died in 1997, a small but vocal
minority criticized her for not focusing more of her energy
on alleviating the causes of poverty, disease and hunger
rather than simply ministering to the sick and dying. But
surely one person doing a lifetime of authentic work like
this leaves behind an indelible message for each of us—that
one person can make a difference.

Some might say that Nelson Mandela wasted *his* life by
spending so much of it in prison, and that he could have
better served his country by acceding to the wishes of his
captors. Yes, it is disheartening to perceive a problem as so
overwhelming that it has no ultimate solution, and yet

where would we be without men and women who had the faith, spirit and soul to press on in the face of overwhelming odds? For one, the entire planet Earth might be under Nazi domination. Polio might still be killing and crippling millions of people. We might still believe that the sun rotates around the earth. One man or one woman who has focus and fierce determination *will* make a difference, but that one person will have to be spiritual to carry out his or her life's work. Without spirituality, people get discouraged and quit when too many obstacles arise.

8. If Other People Are Poor, Sick, Troubled or Dying, It's Their Own Fault—It's Not My Problem (Narcissism, Egocentrism, Inability to Love or Experience Empathy and Compassion)

The easy way to address this spiritual barrier is to come at it from a purely biological point of view. We are social animals just like baboons and wolves. Scientifically speaking, this means that without each other, we would not have survived as long as we have. By pooling our collective intelligences, we improve our survivability exponentially. One person is good at building boats out of trees, one is good at plotting a course by watching the stars move around in the sky, another is good at growing things, and yet another is a born mediator, which would be no small skill on an open-ocean voyage to an unknown destination in a cramped dugout canoe.

That's the scientific explanation. The spiritual one is that we are empathic, loving creatures who are driven by two urges. One is to be separate, to build, create, conquer and exert our wills on creation. The other is to join socially, emotionally and spiritually with each other not only for our common good, but because it is part of our identities as human beings to want to do so. When a society is barely surviving under conditions of prolonged starvation, what often happens is that it *is* every man for himself. There are simply not enough resources for people to do anything but fend for themselves, with one exception. People who have a religious and/or spiritual orientation are able to make ethical, caring decisions and act accordingly for longer periods of time, and under more severe conditions, than people who don't. What is the function of religion if not to help us rise above our own human limitations and animal instincts? Every human being experiences loss, tragedy and limitations. Each of us will experience hard times across our lifespans. Each of us will sorely need others now and then. Spiritual people understand and embrace this fact of life.

9. Faster Is Better; More Is Better (Excessiveness)

In *Democracy In America*, written in 1835, Alexis de Tocqueville described Americans as "forever brooding over advantages they do not possess. . . . It is strange to see with what feverish ardor the Americans pursue their own welfare, and to watch the vague dread that constantly torments them lest they should not have chosen the shortest path which may lead to it." We Americans pride ourselves in how clever and innovative we are. We lead the world in space exploration, computer technology, medicine and fast-food restaurants. We work long hours. We also consume most of the world's natural resources even though we only comprise about 5 percent of the world's population. Growing up amidst this kind of affluence can give a child a very distorted feel for the rest of humanity. Imagine how cut off that child must be. It's almost like growing up in Disneyland instead of in the real world. Growing up in affluence without a sense of proportion about it can cause a child to be ungrateful and unhappy rather than compassionate for the rest of humanity. No wonder so many of us believe that more is better. A tragic saying circulating around the country is: "The one who dies with the most toys wins." Wins what? How could anyone with that philosophy of life ever develop any spirituality? It's difficult to imagine.

And *is* faster better? Certainly in many cases it is. We'd rather fly to San Francisco than go by covered wagon. We'd rather have a cavity in our teeth drilled out by a high-speed drill than by one of those painfully slow models from the 1950s. But is zipping through the drive-thru at McDonald's and scarfing down a hamburger as you race along the freeway your idea of an aesthetic experience? Or can it be an aesthetic, even spiritual experience to savor a seven-course meal prepared and presented with artistic care, eaten slowly, and accompanied by warm conversation among old and dear friends? Is it better to read the *Reader's Digest* condensed version of a great literary work, or might you be missing something by doing it this way? Surely there must be some value in occasionally taking something in through all of your slow-speed input devices (a.k.a. "the five senses") and savoring it rather than downloading it via a serial port implanted on the back of your skull.

10. Distractions Are Better Than Feelings (Addiction, Fear of Intimacy, Inability to Experience Life at Its Fullest)

It is often said that we have an addictive culture. When you get past the biochemical bases for addiction, what you're left with are the emotional and social bases. Addictions begin as a useful numbing of uncomfortable feelings. There is nothing inherently wrong with going home at night after a particularly tense day at work and then zoning out in front of the television or having a stiff drink. Our brains have the capacity for distraction for a reason. Distractions help us to prevent overload. The problem enters when the occasional distraction for the occasional bad day turns into a routine. A couple of stiff drinks a few times a year become several stiff drinks on a regular basis—or a huge binge every once in awhile. Or watching television mindlessly for a couple of hours becomes watching television mindlessly for several hours every day.

Imagine, if you can, the kind of intimacy that exists in a household where one, several or all of the family members watch television compulsively. Imagine the disruption to intimacy that occurs if one family member is mildly high on some chemical all the time. How is it different to interact with this person? This family member may argue that she only has a slight "buzz" on and that she's more pleasant and fun to be with when she's "up" a little bit. But isn't it different? People who live with someone who is always a little high will tell you that it's enormously different, and that they feel "crazy" because it's such a subtle difference that the addict can keep arguing that it's a good thing rather than a bad one.

An addiction is something that blocks feelings on a regular basis. Because it's impossible to block one feeling and not have others affected, this means that the emotional life of the addicted person is blunted or distorted. Because deeper intimacy between people requires an emotional connection, an addiction therefore blocks intimacy. Addicts will often tell you that their addiction makes them *more* intimate by relaxing them, opening up their boundaries, or by making them more socially comfortable. But this is only true at a superficial level. Interacting with a person in an addicted state only allows for superficial intimacy. That's why it's so boring and unfulfilling if you're at a party where everyone but you is drinking or using other chemicals. They all think they're being intimate and feeling close, but they really aren't, and you're the only one who knows it. They may know it the next day when they feel embarrassed or can't remember all that "intimacy," but by then, the party's over.

If spirituality requires the ability to have a relationship with other human beings, and to be able to appreciate and stand before the ineffable in the universe, then of course being addicted will surely interfere with a person's spirituality. We often use the example of a tornado coming directly into an addict's house. The addict defiantly shakes his fist at the tornado and yells, "Get away from my house," and in his narcissistic delusions of grandeur and power actually believes that this will save his house. The spiritual person next door looks at the tornado, says to himself, "This is much more powerful than me," and then heads for the basement. After the tornado has passed, having destroyed both houses, the spiritual person crawls out of his basement and then searches for the body so that he can have a proper funeral for his addicted neighbor.

Living all of life, including its sorrows and disappointments as well as its joys and triumphs, is one of the primary gifts of being spiritual. It allows unparalleled depth and appreciation. It lets us be grateful for what we have as well as for what has been taken from us, and by doing so, enables us to have joy. We can't do any of these things very well if we are actively practicing an addiction.

11. If I Let Other People See the True "Me," They'll Hurt Me (Fear of Intimacy)

When we first interview a new client, one of the questions we ask is, "Are you satisfied with the amount and kinds of support in your life?" As people progress in the therapy process, one of the most significant changes that occurs is a deepening of their capacity for intimacy. Putting all jargon aside, this simply means that they are able to share deeper and deeper parts of themselves with others, without losing their identities in the process. One of the timeless paradoxes of human experience is that the one thing we long for the most is also one of the things that frightens us the most: *others seeing us*. For obvious reasons, the more of ourselves that we share with others, the more exposed we become to criticism and rejection, which are the psychological equivalents of a life-threatening physical attack.

The truth is that if you *do* let other people see the real you, *some* of them *will* hurt you. Therein lies the dilemma. If you protect your "self" by remaining closed to other human beings, you will be safe from harm in one way, but you will be so isolated and alone that you will wind up hurting yourself very deeply in another way.

Consider what many people experience in therapy and support groups. When a woman sits in a circle for the first time with other women and declares, "My name is Jill, and I have breast cancer," something spiritual happens among those women that will change her and them forever. When a man declares for the first time that he was beaten up by his father when he was a little boy, and weeps genuine tears as he speaks, or when the guy next to him shares that his gambling has nearly destroyed his marriage and family, you can almost see the spiritual connections forming, strengthening and then deepening among group members. If you look closely, you can almost see rays of light extending across the room from person to person. When someone takes the risk to share parts of himself that have shame and fear attached to them, and if he shares these parts in a safe environment, something happens that is ineffable. It is this indescribable feeling of warmth, connection, relief and inner peace that constitutes a major part of spirituality.

We can all go to the mountaintop and pray by ourselves, which is good. But until we also take the beautiful, gracious risk of letting others "see" us, we are only running on half of our spiritual cylinders.

Teach Your Children Well

Many of us know what we can do to help our children become more spiritual, but we sometimes have a difficult time doing it because it requires change and commitment on our part. Developing more humility and trust, taking time for living, learning to appreciate the value of struggle, and facing our own isolationism, narcissism, selfishness, fear of intimacy or unresolved anger about religious abuse in childhood takes courage, effort and risk. Certain kinds of clinical depression *are* best treated with medication, but facing life with realism *and* hope requires that we grow up, and growing up is hard to do.

It is easy to say that many parents are so immature nowadays that it is as if children are raising children. But this has always been true to some extent, and always will be, because none of us is ever fully mature or fully healthy. The question isn't, "Who is grown up enough to raise children?" A better question is, "How can I grow up some more, and when will I be ready to do it?" One of the more joyous discoveries we have made over the years is that it is never too late for a parent to risk growing some more, and if a parent takes the risk, it will always impact his or her children positively. We say this recognizing that it's risky to say "never" and "always," but we have seen the positive outcomes so many times, across so many different chronological ages, stages and circumstances, that it is a pretty safe risk for us to take.

7

Be Your Child's Best Friend

No Guts, No . . .

H. Jackson Brown, the author of the bestselling *Life's Little Instruction Book*, wrote another little book based in large part on the wise teachings of his own father. We keep a copy of *A Father's Book of Wisdom* in our waiting room and receive numerous positive comments about it from people who have browsed through it. One of the quotations from his father goes like this: "Fathers are pals nowadays because they don't have the guts to be fathers." (p. 95) That's a very powerful quote, and interestingly enough, most of the people who read it simply nod quietly in agreement. When men and women are actually in our office doing their therapy work, part of the hard work they do consists of teasing out all the nuances and implications of a quote like this. Parents know there's a measure of truth to this quote, but they aren't always sure what it means in actual practice.

The health of the relationship between parents and children is not particularly easy to pin down, a fact that is further complicated by the remarkable diversity among parenting styles across cultures. If nothing else, it is safe to say that human beings are adaptive and resilient enough that any number of relationship structures can be healthy, within reason. In some cultures, babies are left in their cribs more than in others. In some, formal rites of passage carry children from one childhood stage to the next; in others, there appear to be no formal rites of passage. Child psychologists will probably debate the question of universally healthy parenting styles for as long as we are still a species on this planet. But that is not to say that there are no guidelines to follow.

Why do so many of us nod with approval when we read a quote like Brown's on the previous page? It must resonate somehow with our personal observations about children in this country. With what is it resonating? We believe it strikes deeply into a gnawing concern that many of us have about the dissolving boundary between parent and child in the United States. Family systems theorists like Salvador Minuchin point out that in a healthy family, a semipermeable boundary exists between parents and children so that while they are connected to each other in intimate ways, they are also separate from each other in appropriate ways. In other words, in a healthy family, somebody is always in charge. When the boundary begins to dissolve, the result is emotional chaos.

Chaos or Isolation Versus Comfort and Safety

Here is another example of where examining the extremes on a continuum can help us all become better parents. When parents and children have a very weak boundary between them, the result is chaos. When there is a very rigid boundary between parents and children, the result is disconnection and isolation. Neither one is healthy. When the boundary between parents and children is clear and flexible, the system functions much better. In some families, the major focus of therapy work is to repair this intergenerational boundary so that children can feel comfortable and safe while still having room to grow up.

Emotional Chaos

If you think emotional chaos could be a problem, you are right. Why would it cause emotional chaos if a dad or mom tried to be a child's pal? Just look around. What is a classroom like when the teacher always tries to be "the nice one"? You know. We're talking about the teacher who is really "loose" and unstructured, and who values being friends with students over teaching them and demonstrating leadership. It feels real good in the beginning, doesn't it? The kids are excited about this "closer" relationship that they get to have with an adult. It makes them feel special and even powerful. A few weeks into the semester, some of the students begin to have doubts about it all. It feels like no one is in charge. The assignments aren't clear. If a few students challenge an assignment, the teacher spends an inordinate amount of time "processing" it with them in an attempt to keep everybody happy. Pretty soon the students are in charge of the classroom. Pretty soon there is chaos.

How about in the workplace? What is it like when you have a vice president, manager or supervisor whose goal is to be your pal? Same thing. At first it feels good. Everybody's real close. It feels warm and fuzzy. One big happy family. Under this kind of management, what happens after the warm fuzzies wear off is much the same as in the classroom. People don't know what they're supposed to do. They don't know how they're being evaluated. Everyone feels good until there's a conflict, and then a whole bunch of people feel stabbed in the back by Mr. or Ms. Nice Guy. This is so, because it is impossible to please everybody. You want your project to continue, the higher-ups don't. Funding will be pulled. But your supervisor has to be the Nice Guy, and so he never really tells you directly, secretly hoping that you'll hear the bad news from someone else. When you do hear it from someone else, you feel like your supervisor set you up behind the scenes, even if he didn't, but he probably did, because he couldn't stand to be clear with you for fear of your getting mad at him.

Children need and desire structure. They don't know how to ask for it directly. In weak systems, they also get seduced by the lack of structure. They get used to it, intoxicated by it, and then they can't let go of the inordinate amount of power they have acquired. The ultimate dilemma for parents and children when it comes to this issue is that they both want to be liked because they love and care about each other, and yet they both need structure. It surely isn't the child's job to provide the structure, and at some unconscious level, children know this. The result isn't very good.

Isolation and Disconnection

At the other extreme are families in which the parents are so separate from the children that there is little warmth or connection between them. These would include parents who are overly stern, rigid, inflexible and authoritarian, as well as those who are simply way too detached. The latter would include stereotypic wealthy families in which the children are raised by a nanny and sent off to boarding school at an early age. Our clients who were raised in this kind of a family often describe their relationship with their parents as that between a low-level employee and the CEO of the corporation—very distant, very formal and with little emotional connection.

There is usually little chance of parents becoming their kids' pals in these kinds of systems. The trade-off is that there is little chance of a relationship developing, either. Unlike in the "pal" system, in one type of rigid system, children know what is expected of them at every turn. If bedtime is 9:00 P.M., the kids go to bed at 9:00 P.M. even if a rare, once-in-a-century meteor shower will be occurring at 10:00 P.M. and it's a Saturday night, and Dad and Mom will be watching it with all of the other adults and children from the neighborhood. Rules are rules, and there are no exceptions. It is a terror about emotional closeness and of accepting the uncontrollable in the universe that underlies this type of parenting style.

Fear is a healthy emotion that gives us crucial information about life. Control is also healthy up to a point, such as in our attempts to control the impact of weather by building structures that keep out the elements. If we didn't fear freezing to death, we wouldn't bother insulating our homes and installing furnaces. Excessive control indicates excessive anxiety and fear, and so although the surface of this kind of family is very orderly, the inner psychology is also in chaos. There is little inner peace.

If They Get Mad, You Won't Shatter

The question we so often hear as parents begin to struggle to repair these intergenerational boundaries is: "How can I alter my relationship with my kids without causing distress?" The simple answer is: "You can't." You can't repair anything in a system without causing distress. Change is distressing to people. On the up side, nobody will break if they have to change now and then. And there is certainly nothing odd about children getting angry at parents when parents say "No." It is natural to get angry when someone denies our requests. It is normal.

Suppose your ten-year-old has been spending literally all of his time with you, being your pal, to the exclusion of learning how to get along with other kids. Suppose you decide to change this. Suppose you are heading out to the nearby lake to take a peaceful walk in solitude, and your ten-year-old starts to join you, but you explain gently that you need some time to yourself to reflect on things. His feelings will be hurt, and then he will get angry at you for turning him down in a situation where you would usually include him. You go on your walk. You return. Perhaps he is pouting. You act as if everything is normal. He continues to pout. You go on with your day. He pouts some more. Finally, you firmly but gently explain that there are times when you need to do things on your own, that you understand his anger, but that the anger won't change this, and that if the pouting continues, you will have to ask him to do it in his room because you aren't going to be punished with sighs and eye-rolling for the rest of the day. You then continue to go about your day. He goes out and pouts some more. Eventually he realizes you aren't going to give in to his pouting, and then he cheers up and decides he'd better go next door to see if the neighbor boy wants to play. This is all normal and natural. Is it distressful for the two of you until the change becomes part of the system? Of course it is. Does that mean you shouldn't make the change? Of course it doesn't.

You may have noticed that this subheading emphasizes that *you* won't shatter if they get mad at you. In our experience, beneath the fear that their children will be hurt by the change is the parents' fear that *they* won't be able to handle the short-term distress of having their children mad at them. Remember that children won't shatter if their parents make changes like this firmly, gently, slowly, but consistently. They just won't shatter, even if you fear that they will.

Examples of Pal Behavior

Sometimes the line between being a warm parent and being a pal isn't crystal clear, so let us go over some examples that we have found are troublesome for some families. You'll probably see where the trouble is right away.

Off to the Country Club

Janie is the apple of her Daddy's eye, which pleases Dad, Janie and Mom, whose father ignored her when she was growing up. Janie goes with Dad everywhere he goes. She especially likes to go to the country club with him and act as his sidekick while he plays bridge with his buddies. She feels like a queen and is an absolute firecracker, as well as a subtle charmer. Everybody loves to have her around, especially Dad's cronies. Janie is now eleven years old, and this has been going on for a long time. It has become part of their family structure with nothing but positive effects as far as anyone can see. When she enters a room, all eyes turn toward her, just like when she first learned to walk and Daddy's face came alive with a celestial radiance. People comment on what a great relationship she has with her father, and her friends are secretly envious of her for all her energy, charm and attention.

What's the Problem?

Many people ask us what could possibly be wrong with being Dad's Princess or Mom's Little Man. It seems like such a natural way to build a child's self-esteem, and we can all think of examples of such children who do, indeed, appear to have gigantic reserves of self-esteem. They are often poised, confident, assertive, high-achieving and the center of attention. So what's the problem? If life were only about achievement and confidence, then there wouldn't *be* a problem. But life is also about relationships, depth and balance. So, let's look at a few likely problem areas.

First of all, while Mom may encourage Janie and Dad to have such a special relationship "because Mom had a poor relationship with her own father," what actually happens is that Mom soon begins to be *justifiably* jealous and resentful of their relationship because it becomes too special and exclusive. Mom is supposed to be the most significant person in Dad's life, not Janie. Mom walks into the living room and Dad may or may not notice her. Janie bounds enthusiastically into the living room and jumps into Daddy's lap, and Daddy beams excitedly. Mom wants to spend an afternoon and evening with Dad because they haven't had a date in weeks, but she has to compete with Janie for Dad's attention; or worse, Dad invites Janie along. Eventually, this arrangement not only gives Janie a distorted sense of herself, but also taints her relationship with her mother. Mom secretly resents Janie and then hates herself for feeling that way, which does terrible damage to her own self-esteem. Mom and Janie have, at best, a strained relationship, robbing them of the joy they could be sharing as life goes on.

Second, if Janie has any brothers or sisters, then the same sort of thing happens here, too. They secretly resent Janie but are highly conflicted in their feelings, which makes them agitated and confused inside. After all, if they secretly resent The Princess, and The King finds out, they might be in worse shape than they already are. So they aspire to be like her in the hopes of winning some of Dad's special attention, but alas, no matter what they try, they can't win. Why not? Because they aren't Janie. If anyone were to raise this issue with Dad or Mom, they would naturally express shock and disbelief, giving example after example of how Dad treats each child in a special way. But if Janie is truly Dad's Pal and Princess, it won't matter what Dad does. The damage will occur anyway. When we work with adults whose brother or sister was The Special One during childhood, invariably a big piece of therapy work centers on the hurt, resentment, guilt and shame that have built up over the decades.

Third, we have to ask what's happening to Dad during all of this. Having a special relationship with your son or daughter is usually easier than having a special relationship with your adult partner, because children are vulnerable and are predisposed to love us because they are so dependent on us. If we treat an adult partner poorly for long enough, they will usually leave us. Children are much less likely to leave. So, all the while that Dad is having this wonderful relationship with Janie, something inside of him is whispering, "This isn't right. You ought to be spending more time with your wife. But she is a grown-up. It's more of a threat." Or, if Dad is simply overcompensating for his own painful childhood, then he is short-changing himself by not facing his pain and working it through. He is actually using Janie to avoid growing up some more, although he would be shocked at first to hear that.

Finally, Janie gets hurt in some unique ways that may not even appear until she is in her twenties or thirties. She literally charges through elementary school, high school and college, the darling of everyone along the way. She goes to graduate school and is again a star. Boys swarm around her because her personality is so infectious, charming and disarming. But as she enters her thirties, subtle indications arise that something has gone awry. Even Janie is becoming aware of it, but after thirty years of being on top of the world the prospect of addressing a personal flaw is too much to bear, and so she just forges ahead into life the way she has always done. Her parents notice that the men with whom she gets involved treat her like a princess.

She dates powerful men who parade around with her on their arm as if she were an accessory until they grow weary of her and turn her in for a newer model; or, she goes out with men who literally have her on a pedestal like a princess, which understandably causes her to despise them after a short while. Being in an adult love relationship requires emerging depth after awhile, and to have depth, you must be willing to look at yourself deeply. Therein lies the crux of the problem. By the time Janie has had a decade or so of unhappy love relationships and is ready to look more deeply at this dynamic, it is almost too painful to acknowledge what has happened to her. When she is finally able to consciously "see" and "feel" what hit her, she must come face-to-face with the fact that being too special is just as bad as not being special enough. And of course, her parents didn't do this maliciously—they thought they were doing the best thing they could. The ambivalence and inner turmoil she experiences are staggering. Fortunately, if she endures the pain of facing this damaging pattern, she will be able to have a good love relationship someday. But not until she faces it.

What to Do Instead

If you or your partner have a vague inkling that this Prince or Princess dynamic has begun, the first thing to do is talk about it calmly and specifically, as in: "Honey, you know, I've been missing our alone time together. Have you noticed the same thing?" The partner has to resist being defensive and take in what you've said, and then mull it over for a few days, not just reject it out of hand. Or a husband could say to his wife, "I really feel sheepish bringing this up, but it's one of those things that could really get in the way if I don't say something now. I'm starting to resent your relationship with Timmy." The wife has to let it in, pay attention and be open to the possibility that her husband is making a valid point.

Of course, if you aren't sure if you're off-base or not, then say so, and suggest that the two of you get some outside advice from someone who isn't just going to put their imprimatur on whatever you do or say. We all know people who will support whatever we say. And we all know how to put just enough spin on a story to make it sound better or worse than it really is. So if you get outside counsel, be sure it's objective.

If you have a pretty solid relationship to begin with, making this mid-course correction will not be a daunting experience. At worst, it will be uncomfortable until the change has been in place for a few weeks. And what changes are we talking about? If you catch it early, they're simple things like consciously paying as much attention to the other kids as to the Special One, or making sure that you and your spouse go out alone regularly without any of the kids. In our Country Club example, it might also include the father going to the country club by himself, or with his wife, and bringing Jamie only when the other children are also included and there is a specific family gathering there.

Doing things to make your marriage special, and to make all of the members of your family feel important, will save your marriage, the Special Child, and the rest of your children from years of confusion and heartache. Please remember that change is uncomfortable and disruptive at first, and that children will not shatter just because you institute changes now and then.

Mom's One of the Gang!

Mrs. Thornton is great. Her teenage son, Bill, and all of his friends, spend a lot of time at their house partly because she is always so friendly, talkative and funny. Bill's friend, Clarence, told his dad that Mrs. Thornton "is just like one of us" at times. She works mornings at a software development firm and is home by 2:30 every afternoon so that she can be there for her children. On many an afternoon she has a whole kitchen full of teenagers whom she feeds and then hangs out with. The teens especially love the fact that she kids and teases and acts more like one of them than like the "typical" parent.

What's the Problem?

Teenagers have two great sayings: "Get a Life!" and "Grow up!" That's the problem. Where are Mrs. Thornton's friends? What is she doing with her life? When did she stop growing up? When she sits at home and waits for her son and his friends to get there so she can be friends with them, the message she sends, like it or not, is, "I don't have any friends. I'm too scared to make adult friends. I'm too scared to even address the problem. I don't have anything else to do with my life when I'm not at work." Does this mean that she should never be home when the kids get back from school? Certainly not. It's very good for children to know that someone will be there after school. It's more about how those after-school interactions go.

When Friday and Saturday nights roll around, dads and moms who are caught in this trap will often say something like, "Oh, you go on out and have fun with your friends. I'm not one bit lonely. I have plenty to do tonight [Like ironing *your* shirts or blouses, which makes you feel even more guilty]. It's just fun for me to see you have fun with your friends [Translation: I'm living my life through you]."

Our adult clients who lived with this pattern recall feeling very guilty and responsible for their dad or mom. Many of them actually chose to stay home on Friday and Saturday nights, saying, "Oh, you know, Dad, I really enjoy staying home on weekends now and then. After all, I'll be all grown up and out of the house before you know it." Sounds pretty good, doesn't it? Loyal child, not out using drugs or experimenting with sex. Just staying at home by the fire with good old Dad or Mom. Except for one thing. They're seething inside with pity and resentment and guilt, but don't know any way out. The only way out is to leave you at home by your pitiful self, or to stay home and resent it. Children are like little air molecules who will swoosh in and fill whatever vacuum they find. If your life is a vacuum, they'll automatically try to rush in and fill it up, no matter *what* you tell them to the contrary

What to Do Instead

The simplest thing to do for this problem is to get a life in addition to your life with your children and their friends. For some, this is a daunting task because of their particular childhood shortages, but it is a task that will be successfully achieved once you put your mind to it. Remember that whenever you tell yourself that you can't do something, or that something will never happen, you can't and it won't. When you look at the task as a challenge that is achievable with effort, then it will be achieved.

People who have a hard time finding other adults to be with often tell us that they simply don't know how, or that they don't know where to look. But if you look around, you will see hundreds upon hundreds of people at every turn. The problem isn't a lack of people, it's usually a lack of know-how coupled with some fear of taking the risk to initiate relationships. We recommend that you begin by telling yourself this: "I will stop relying on my children for the *adult* support that I need, even if my children are now adults. My first step is to begin putting myself in places where I am likely to meet other adults, even though this makes me uncomfortable. My initial goal is nothing more

than to put myself in places where I may meet other adults.
I will continue with this goal until I am somewhat comfortable, and then I will create the next goal of actually
developing a couple of ongoing friendships."

We have literally seen hundreds of people struggle successfully with this problem. It is not easy at first. After all,
fear of getting hurt by others is universal. We watch as a
man chooses to hang around to socialize after church on
Sunday for the first time since childhood. We privately
cheer as a woman volunteers to help a couple of the other
moms tutor kids at school. We feel joy when a couple signs
up to take ballroom dancing classes on Friday nights, knowing that they will have to meet and interact with other
adults, and perhaps for the first time in many years, get
close to each other. There are groups out there for almost
everything nowadays. There are ski clubs, photography
clubs, singles groups, parents without partners, divorced
and separated Catholics, and clubs for people who are fasci-
nated by tenth-century Celtic architecture. If you have an
identifiable addiction, like alcoholism or compulsive spending, then there are free self-help groups in nearly every town
in the United States. In other words, take yourself by the
hand and just get out there and do it.

If you are so scared of being hurt that you aren't able to
do any of the above, then get yourself into a therapy group.
A good therapy group facilitated by a competent therapist
is probably the safest place to learn relationship skills if your
needs and issues are appropriate for such a group. If you are
not a candidate for group therapy because of your particular
personal issues, then working on a one-to-one basis with a

good therapist is also an excellent way to gradually move into the adult social world. In our men's and women's therapy groups, we have worked with some of the finest, brightest, most competent people we have ever encountered. You'd be surprised by the number of wonderful people who have steered their lives in better directions by participating in groups.

Poor Dad

Fred Thompson has been married to Helen for seventeen years. They have three children, ages sixteen, fourteen and eleven. Helen is the one in the partnership who is more structured and intense, and she has suffered on and off with low-grade depression for many years. She has spells of irritability that erupt into rage fairly regularly. Fred is the gentler of the two, and he tries to balance Helen's negative spells by being especially flexible and friendly with his children. He never confronts Helen with her behavior because he knows it will just make her angrier.

Sometimes, though, Helen's negative spells get so painful that Fred discusses the problem with his sixteen-year-old son, Alex. While sitting around their campfire one night during their annual backpacking trip in the mountains, Fred says to Alex, "Sometimes I get so frustrated and down about your mother's behavior. I hate to say it, but there are even times when I wish I hadn't married her." Alex listens intently and sympathetically because he knows all too well what Dad is talking about. He feels a whole range of emotions, but the prevailing one is of warmth and closeness and connectedness to his father. He feels relieved that someone is actually putting words on a problem that plagues him as well. He feels powerful and grown up because his father is sharing these personal reflections with him, in private, man-to-man. He feels angry at Mom for making their lives so uncomfortable, but guilty that he is listening to Dad talk about her behind her back. He especially feels sorry for Dad, seeing as how Dad is such a nice guy and Mom is so difficult to live with. All-in-all, it is a very powerful emotional experience for Alex, and it feels good to Fred to have finally unburdened himself with his son, in such a special environment for the two of them.

What's the Problem?

By now, you're probably getting the picture. The problem here is very similar to the other examples above. Fred is *using* Alex for something. Because it feels good at one level, Alex is actually seduced into it. And because Mom's behavior directly affects Alex, there is a special investment on top of it. But put yourself in Alex's position for just thirty seconds. How would *you* feel if your father told you that there were times he wished he hadn't married your mother? You're caught right in the middle. You'll feel conflicted. You may even get knots in your stomach, have anxiety problems and feel tremendous guilt. After all, by simply *listening* to Dad, you are somehow betraying Mom. It's a pretty painful picture.

But what if you are twenty-seven years old when this starts happening? With a couple of specific exceptions, the problem still remains, for the same reasons. You get caught in the middle, and it feels "icky." The only times we can think of when this might need to happen would be if Mom were incapacitated, as in the case of Alzheimer's disease, or if she were heavily in denial about some *serious* self-destructive behavior, like driving her car while drunk, or being suicidal. Otherwise, it just isn't fair to use children this way because the bond it creates between you and your child is *very intense* and leads to all kinds of emotional and intimacy problems for your child later, when he or she is in adulthood.

What to Do Instead

Parents and children should have a clear, flexible boundary between them. This means that there are certain things that parents should do with each other or with other adults, not with children. Fred Thompson is faced with a challenging situation: The woman he loves gets angry a lot and Fred has a tough time dealing with it. He rarely steps up to the plate for fear of inciting her anger even more. And so he has taken the path of least resistance and the one that he unconsciously believes is the best path. He chooses to be "nice," and then on occasion he draws his kids into it and inadvertently causes them to take sides by merely listening to him complain about Mom.

Clearly, Fred needs to say: "I will no longer put my kids in the middle by talking to them about Mom. I will find other adults outside of my immediate family to share my burdens with if need be, and I will get help in learning how to work directly with Helen in new ways that will eventually strengthen our marriage rather than hurting it." If he takes this higher path, Fred will encounter some rough terrain along the way, at least in the beginning. He will probably have to face whatever it is that caused him to be afraid to step up to the plate in the first place, and then he will have to try out and then practice new ways of contributing to the strength of his marriage. And just to be sure we're all on the same wavelength, remember that for those of you who still see problems like these in black and white instead of technicolor, we can assure you that there are scores of alternatives between business-as-usual and divorce.

The Twelve-Steppers

Susan and Tom are both recovering alcoholics who grew up in unhealthy families. Susan experienced regular physical battery as a child; Tom was viciously criticized by his parents when he was growing up. They both entered chemical dependency treatment at approximately the same time and have been sober now for two years. As part of their ongoing therapy work, they have been examining their childhood abuse issues, which has helped them separate what happened to them as children from how they can choose to act as adults, in the present.

Because they are fairly new to all of this, and because they are beginning to see how strongly they were affected by their childhoods, their anxiety about their children being affected by ongoing family pain is pretty high. In the hopes of heading off this intergenerational pain, they enthusiastically share with their children a good part of what they are learning about their own lives. Without even asking, their children have become well-versed in the emotional histories of their two parents. They have also learned how twelve-step programs work, the dangers of chemical abuse and how to spot co-dependency. They even talk about all of this among themselves now, which makes their parents feel like they have really accomplished something.

What's the Problem?

First of all, that much detail isn't necessary. Kids don't want or need to know that much stuff. Second, without knowing it, by sharing all that detail so frequently, Susan and Tom are transmitting all of their anxiety to their children, which is putting the kids at greater risk for addictions later on, not less. Third, by talking *about* life more than just living it, they aren't really teaching their kids healthy intimacy. They could teach their kids a lot more by simply living their sober lives more and more graciously with every passing year. Fourth, it is an intergenerational boundary violation to share too much parental detail with children at too early of an age. Fifth, lecturing our children with this stuff just pushes them away, which also sets them up for problems later on. When they need someone to go to with their problems, they will be less likely to go to Tom and Susan because of all the lectures.

What to Do Instead

Going to the other extreme is not the answer. Hiding everything from our children doesn't help. If Tom and Susan never drink alcohol anymore, what should they say if their kids *ask* them about it? They can say, "We're in recovery now, so we don't drink. It was beyond our power to manage it, so we stopped drinking and started going to AA meetings instead. We feel so much better now." It's that simple. Have a little faith, Tom and Susan. Don't project your anxiety onto your kids. They'll have enough of their own as they grow up. The way to go is to be matter-of-fact, do your best to stay sober, and be prepared to answer your children's questions if they eventually ask. And they probably will, if you haven't pushed them away with your lectures.

Remember that our kids are not us. They are separate people. They won't be nearly as interested in your problems as you are. When it becomes relevant for them, if you've been open and comfortable, they'll ask. But it may not be until they're in their twenties, thirties or even later. In the meantime relax, have a nice cold glass of lemon ice water and watch the sunset. Life is great, and if life is great, your kids will be fine. After all, children learn what they watch, not what you tell them.

8

Fail to Give Your Child Structure

A Brief Lesson About Structure

We know from the work of people like Jean Piaget, Erik Erikson, Jerome Bruner, Jane Loevinger and many others that children learn internal structure and discipline by first experiencing *external* structure. The sequence is quite simple. External structure first. The child gradually internalizes that external structure. Then internal structure forms. It's as easy as 1-2-3.

But that's not all. Internal structure is acquired in an identifiable sequence and this fact has not gone unnoticed in the critical field of impulse control. So, here's how it works. Two Russian psycholinguists, Luria and Vygotsky, spent years studying how children's inner speech develops and how children eventually use it to control their own behavior. In explaining their theory David McNeill wrote:

> *All control is a matter of following instructions, either external or internal. Self- or internal control depends on the development of inner speech, and inner speech in turn derives from socialized speech. Self-control is therefore preceded genetically by external control. (p. 1128)*

This is fairly easy to grasp. Parents give directions to children such as, "Put the toy in the box," or "Watch for cars before you cross the street." Children hear these attempts to provide structure and direction. Children hear these directions some more. Eventually children say these directions to themselves. Voila! Children can control their own behavior by talking to themselves!

Then along came Harvard psychologist Lawrence Kohlberg, who put children's private speech into four developmental stages. In stage one, children's private speech has no control function—it simply consists of animal noises, playing with words, repetitive sounds and so forth. You know how this sounds. Your little one is sitting on the floor playing with a wooden block that he's pretending is an airplane. He makes airplane noises. You crack up and remark on how cute he is. He's yours, after all. You get to do that. But of course, in terms of language controlling behavior, there isn't any of that going on here. During this stage, children's language has no control over their behavior whatsoever. They're just practicing making sound effects for their play.

In stage two, children talk out loud but they just address nonhuman objects or describe what it is they are doing, for example, "I'm jumping up and down! I'm jumping up and down!"

In stage three, children talk out loud but their speech definitely has a regulatory function. This is a crucial stage in children's development, and is, we hope, greeted with excitement and enthusiasm by parents. As you watch and listen to your children using this kind of speech, be aware that you are witnessing one of the miracles of human development because what is happening is that your children are beginning to regulate their own behavior using the medium of language. It is the beginning of something profound. What you will observe, by the way, is your children saying things like this, out loud, but to themselves: "I have to put this block over here because it's gonna fall if I try to put it there. Yes. That's it. Now I can take that other block and put it on top of this one. Good. It's starting to look like a house."

In stage four, children engage in what are called inaudible mutterings. At this stage, we can see that they are talking to themselves privately, internally, because their lips may be moving and they may be making very quiet statements that we can't quite make out.

If you think about it for a moment, the above sequence makes a lot of sense. If you are having trouble imagining what is going on in each of these stages just remember that we *all* engage in *all four* of these types of speech as adults, too. It's just that we do a lot more of the stage four type of inner dialogue than would a young child. Observe yourself the next time you are faced with a difficult problem to solve. Notice that you are talking silently to yourself (stage four), and that at times, especially if the problem is very difficult, you may catch yourself talking out loud (stage three). What you may also be figuring out is that this four-stage developmental sequence gives us a very concrete road map of how to help people gain control of themselves based on the normal way that children learn it in the first place.

We'll return to this in a moment, but for now we'll just note that in the early 1970s, a young psychologist named Donald Meichenbaum was reading all of this research and realized that these ideas might have a direct bearing on helping impulsive children become more reflective. A lot of people, including one of the current authors, were studying reflection-impulsivity in children back in the 1970s; Meichenbaum's application of Luria's, Vygotsky's and Kohlberg's psycholinguistic discoveries was considered quite elegant and brilliant at the time.

Yippee-Ki-Ay (Expletive Deleted)

Now, if you're still wondering why we feel children's development of private speech is so profound, let's use a really practical and striking example. Imagine a grown man hurtling down the highway at seventy miles an hour. It's midnight. The traffic has finally thinned a little bit. Suddenly, a red Porsche appears from nowhere, cuts in front of him causing him to panic and flinch for a split-second, and then roars on down that ribbon of highway. Many people who experience this kind of thing will swear on a stack of Bibles that the only emotion they feel at that moment is *anger*. But we'll bet every cent we have that when this happens on the freeway or anywhere else for that matter, the first emotion *every* human being feels is *fear*. We're all wired up the same in that respect.

So, you feel fear first. How do you know? Pay attention to your body. When you, for a split-second, get cut off on the freeway and a near-accident occurs, you will notice your heart rate and blood pressure increase, your respiration becomes more rapid and shallow, and if you were hooked up to an electroencephalogram (EEG), we'd be able to see your brain waves screaming out. If we had a measure of your galvanic skin response (GSR), that would show the fear, too. This all occurs in the first instant. Then in many people, the rage comes pouring in like an El Niño-driven Pacific Coast rainstorm. In another lightning-fast instant, our so-called grown man presses the gas pedal to the floor, grits his teeth, makes an obscene hand gesture, leans on the horn, aims straight at the rear-end of the Porsche and reaches for the gun in his glove compartment.

He screams "Yippee-ki-ay (expletive deleted)" just like Bruce Willis in *Die Hard*, and then he starts firing. Hooray. Another sad case of someone shooting up the freeways. Except for one thing. This is an ordinary person. He's the guy next door. Your college professor. Your boss. Your most valued employee. He's your brother. Your husband. Your father. And now he's going to prison for a long, long time. All because he forgot how, or never really knew how, to use his own internal speech to control his behavior. Do you see why talking to yourself is so important?

Just in case you're still not sure, here's what should have

happened. Pay close attention. It may save you and your family's lives someday.

1. The Porsche cuts him off.
2. He feels fear.
3. The anger wells up inside of him.
4. He says to himself, "Back off. Back off. Foot off the gas pedal. Go easy. Don't do it. Maybe that guy's wife is dying in the ER, and he's trying to get to her side. Back off. Relax. Breathe. Calm. Stay calm."
5. He drives home, crawls into bed with his wife, cuddles up to her, says a prayer of gratitude that he and his loved ones are alive and well, and then falls peacefully asleep.

Not everyone has trouble controlling their impulses on the freeway, of course. Some people rage at their employees, or at their spouses and children. Some rage at the officials at children's sporting events, which is apparently enough of a national problem to warrant a special *20/20* news segment all its own. Some rage at airline ticket agents, at department store clerks, or at their next-door neighbors. And impulse control isn't always about anger, either. If you tend to jump to conclusions, have trouble solving problems systematically, or blow things out of proportion, this sequence adapted from the work of Meichenbaum will be very effective.

Impulse Control: Mischel's Marshmallows and Meichenbaum's Self-Talk

It is sad to encounter a very bright individual who lacks emotional intelligence. Sad, too, that our culture so overvalues academic intelligence that by the time a person is all grown up and realizes he or she lacks emotional intelligence, it's a lot more work to acquire it.

So let's go back to Stanford's Walter Mischel and his experiment designed to test four-year-olds' ability to delay gratification. If we want to raise happy, competent children, we need to ensure that they develop some emotional intelligence. One of the key components of emotional intelligence is the ability to delay gratification. But the ability to delay gratification is highly dependent upon the degree to which a child has developed internal structure and verbal control of his own behavior. Part of the way children learn to have internal structure is (1) if their parents are grown up enough to provide them with *external* structure along the way. The other part is (2) if someone is able to teach them to develop internal structure and to make effective use of "inner self-talk."

In his initial research way back in the 1970s, Donald Meichenbaum found that children could learn to control and improve their problem-solving performance by being taught to use their silent self-talk effectively. What's more, he found that this training was especially helpful for children who were impulsive or were diagnosed with attention deficit hyperactivity disorder (ADHD). Based on the findings of Luria and Vygotsky, Meichenbaum designed a training procedure which follows the natural developmental sequence of self-regulating speech. He was very clear in stressing that the way parents and teachers usually explain things to children is terribly ineffective, albeit well-intentioned. It is *not* particularly helpful to lecture at children. It isn't helpful to *tell* kids how to think and process.

Show, Don't Tell

What *does* work very well is if we *show* rather than tell. When it comes to having internal structure and impulse control, this is pretty easy once you get the hang of it. Meichenbaum's early studies involved helping children perform better on a task developed by Harvard's Jerome Kagan, in which they had to look at a standard figure at the top and then find the identical figure among several alternatives below it. On this Matching Familiar Figures Test (MFF), all but one of the alternatives has some minor detail that has been changed from the original, as you can see in the authors' rendition in figure 8.1.

FIGURE 8.1

ITEM TYPICAL OF THE MATCHING FAMILIAR FIGURES TEST

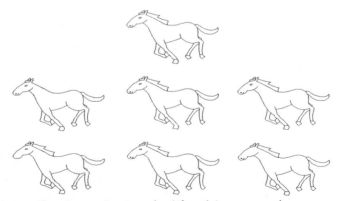

Most of us have done tasks like this at one time or another and find that the best way to attack the problem is to look at one feature of the standard figure and then systematically compare it to each of the alternatives, eliminating alternatives as you go along, until you're left with the correct answer. As Professor Kagan (1966) discovered, about two-thirds of us tackle this kind of problem in one of two ways: (1) we either take our time, do it systematically and make few errors, or (2) we rush it, do it chaotically and make a lot of errors. The former are called reflectives, the latter are impulsives.

Here's how Meichenbaum helped those impulsive little kids do a lot better on this task. First, he modeled the effective strategy by talking out loud as he solved the problem, like this: "Okay, let's see. I think the best way will be to start with the head of the horse, and then I'll look at each of the alternatives, one at a time, and when I find one that doesn't match, I'll put one of my fingers on it. That way I won't have to waste time looking at that one anymore. Yes. Okay. Take your time. Oops, I missed that one. That's okay. Just slow it down a little. Good. That's right. I'm doing fine. This is kind of fun. Stay calm. Don't get too nervous. Now, I'll take the next feature and compare it." We'll stop here, but be aware that Meichenbaum didn't. If you were doing this for real, you'd want to model the entire problem from start to finish. It's important to take that part seriously.

Next, he instructed the child to do one of the problems on his own while talking himself through it, out loud. Practice makes perfect, and of course, since children first use overt speech to control their own behavior, it makes sense to have them say it out loud first. After the child did this, he was asked to do another problem, but this time he was to talk to himself very quietly so that Meichenbaum could barely hear it. And lastly, the child was instructed to solve one of the problems while talking to himself *silently*. Voila! What a brilliant training procedure. The results were stunning. The impulsive children performed almost as well as the reflective ones as a result of the training, whereas the control group did not improve at all.

Captain, or Crew?

Now you know how children learn to use their inner speech to control and regulate their behavior. The other piece of this rests on the consistency of parents when it comes to setting and enforcing rules. In our experience, both as parents and as psychologists, it is far more effective for parents to have a few rules that they enforce consistently rather than a lot of rules that they enforce chaotically. Based on our discussions about inner speech and external social control, it is probably clear that the cumulative effect of parents having tons of rules without enforcing them consistently can be quite severe. Widespread inconsistency prevents the growth of that inner structure that we need in order to be civilized human beings. Disorders of impulse control have become some of the top mental health problems in this nation over the past decade.

How can we possibly expect our kids to have internal structure, self-discipline and self-regulatory skills if we don't have any? It is so sad to watch children who live in these kinds of circumstances. The system has deteriorated so much that the household is in a near-constant state of agitation and emotional chaos. The parents believe that their children are bad. Children are running amok and can't figure out why they disappoint everyone. Everybody is miserable and nobody is sailing with an intact rudder. Who is in charge of the ship? The cocaptains? Or the crew?

Did you ever wonder why it is so common for parents to bring children into therapy to get fixed, only to find the therapist asking the parents to continue in therapy without the children present? If the parents aren't the captains of the ship, then the crew will be in a state of emotional mutiny. Having scores of piddly rules and little enforcement of any of them is a symptom of something. It is a marker, a sign, an indicator, a red flag, the tip of an iceberg. It shouts "Something is wrong!" The saddest part of this scenario is to see parents who are angry at their children for being little monsters when the children are only responding to a system that's been chaotic for years and years.

The structures we grow up in are the ones we internalize. If you grow up in one kind of American family, you may learn that no matter what you do you can hire an attorney and get out of it. You may also learn that filing a lawsuit is a very good way to deal with the everyday setbacks encountered by all human beings. If you grow up in England or Ireland you'd be much less likely to learn these things, but perhaps more likely to learn to be civil to others. It all depends. If your parents let you swear, talk back and be rude to them—if there was too much familiarity between you and them—then you may grow up having a very hard time suppressing your impulses when, say, you are talking to your boss. Without an internal structure that says, "Communicate with superiors respectfully," you might just find yourself getting fired from one job after another, all the while feeling "wronged," "misunderstood" and "unfairly judged." It's sad when we hear someone tell us that they've been unfairly judged, when in fact, they've been hopelessly inappropriate.

Empathy is not the same as sympathy. Parents who have empathy are able to recognize that even if they wanted to give their children everything and let their children get away with everything, it would harm their children. And so despite their occasional pangs of guilt, grown-up parents value structure and help their children create order out of chaos, both in the home, and inside of themselves via their own emotional lives.

Our Recommendations

There are two broad categories to discuss here. One is how to help your children develop self-control—impulse control and delay of gratification—through private speech, and the other is how to create a home that has enough structure so that children come to value it, but not so much that they come to hate it and reject it entirely.

Self-Control

As outlined above, Donald Meichenbaum has demonstrated pretty conclusively that the best way to teach this is to (1) have self-control yourself and thereby model it for your children, and (2) teach it directly using the method that grew out of his research. This method, by the way, is the way many excellent parents already do their teaching. Don't lecture your children or tell them a strategy. Take the strategy that *you* use internally and talk it out, out loud, as you go through the task you're trying to teach. If you feel uncomfortable or awkward doing this at first, practice it with your partner or a friend or alone in front of a mirror. Don't let any embarrassment stop you. This teaching will help your kids grow up to be emotionally healthy.

Here's another example. Suppose you wanted to help your child learn a way to troubleshoot problems that crop up in relationships. But you don't want to solve his particular problem for him. That would be infantilizing. And it wouldn't help your child learn to transfer this skill to other situations. You immediately toss out the thought of giving her advice. So you and your partner do a little role-play instead. The statements in italics are what each person might be thinking in the actual situation, but during the role-play each person actually says these things out loud so that the child can see and hear their inner dialogue. We chose the following example because while it seems like a silly thing to fight about, these are the very kinds of things that people fight about—everyday things. If it seems too mundane, feel free to visualize your own example.

Frank: *I think she borrowed my favorite pen and forgot to return it. I don't want to put her on the defensive, but I need to find out if she knows where my pen is. This is such a sore spot in our relationship—her misplacing my personal belongings. I'll ask her in as neutral a tone as I can muster.* Susan, have you seen my favorite pen anywhere? I can't seem to find it.

Susan: *Oops! I think I used it yesterday when I was in a hurry. He doesn't sound mad. It's probably safe to 'fess up. I'll let him know that I didn't mean any harm, but that I'm willing to own my mistake, and stop what I'm doing so I can help look for it.* Uh . . . yes . . . I was in a terrible hurry yesterday when I grabbed it to write a note. I'm really sorry. Here, I'll look for it right now.

Frank: *Oh, good. We don't have to fight about what happened to it. That was nice of her to offer to drop everything and look for it. She's right in the middle of something, though. Maybe she can just point me in the general direction of the pen.* Oh, good. I thought I'd left it at the grocery store when I wrote out a check. Don't stop what you're doing, but do you have a rough idea of where it might be?

Susan: Let me think for a second. I was heading toward the garage when the phone rang. It was the doctor calling to change Tim's appointment. I jotted a note and then . . . Wait a minute. . . . I had my purse with me. Let me look. . . . *I think that's where it is. This would be great if it's here.* Nope. It's not here. Oh, honey. I'm really sorry.

Frank: *She really looks genuinely apologetic, and I make mistakes like that when I'm in a hurry. Maybe we'd better just let it go for now. It won't hurt me to let go of something temporarily and have faith that it will show up.* That's okay. I'm sure it will turn up. Let's not waste any more time right now. I'd rather spend the time with you.

Susan: *Geeeeeeze, that was nice of him.* Oh, thanks, Frank. Let's all sit down together and have dinner, and then you and I can cuddle up by the fire and watch *60 Minutes*.

Frank: *This feels really good.* Sounds like a good plan to me!

Of course, not only is it fun for your child to watch you role-playing this, it is also an invaluable lesson in conflict resolution *from the inside out.* Children don't forget lessons that are taught this way because they're fun, they're real, they're emotionally complex, they're helpful and they have healthy emotional content.

Structure and Rules

When a system is in chaos, you can enter it from almost any door and if you focus on making one small change and holding that change no matter what, it will eventually calm the chaos and allow more structure to emerge. If your family is out of control, if you have more and more rules, more and more nagging, less and less compliance from your children, more frequent headaches and emotional blow-ups, then you are ready for a change. Go somewhere quiet and then reflect on all of your rules, regulations and expectations, and those of your partner or spouse and then write them out on a sheet of paper.

You may discover that you have so many picky rules that it is embarrassing, but be sure to include every last one of them. The idea here is to see if the system has a ton of rules, many of them tiny and silly, and none of which is enforced with much consistency. When you are finished, look at the paper with your partner and notice what you feel. Embarrassment? Fear because of the chaos? Anger because the kids aren't complying with any of your requests? Okay. Put the paper safely away. Now go do something else for the rest of the day.

After waiting at least twenty-four hours, pick up the
paper again and pick *one* item from the list. Pick a small
one, perhaps. An easy one. Pick one that you know you can
be successful with. This may scare you at first. "But what
about the rest of them?" you might ask. "Patience," we
reply. You must agree between the two of you that this is
the one rule you will both focus on for the next few *weeks*.
Next, you must agree that you are going to let the other
ones go for now. You aren't going to say anymore about
them to your kids. No more nagging, haranguing, lecturing
or threatening. None of that has been effective in the past,
and besides, if you want to regain your power in the system
you will have to reset all the registers to zero, so to speak,
before you can exert influence again. In other words, they
don't listen to you at all when you constantly ask them to
remove their shoes from the foyer, so stop doing it for a few
weeks. The silence will be so much louder than the nagging.
Who knows what might happen all on its own?

Next, do the initial setup for a behavior modification program (we describe the details of this kind of process in chapter 10) for the kids regarding this one item on the list. If it's
putting their own dishes in the dishwasher after each use so
that there are never any dishes in the sink or laying around
the house, then create the program around that. Define all
of your terms and time limits precisely. How long can a dish
"lay around" before a consequence is applied to the person
leaving it there? Five minutes? Ten minutes? Before the
child leaves the area to go out or off to his room? Figure out
consequences that you hope will work. Remember to use
rewards wherever possible. For example, if your teenager

gets the dishes in the dishwasher 80 percent of the time in a seven-day period, he gets something. Then it's fair to build in a negative consequence like losing a privilege if his performance drops below 80 percent.

It's that simple. Pick one rule rather than many. Agree on a way to enforce it fairly. Include something positive for good behavior. *And then follow through!* If you are one of those people who is convinced that struggle is bad, you probably have your work cut out for you, so get going. You can do it. Struggle is good.

Structure or Chaos: It's Up to You

You have probably gathered by now that we believe that without structure in a child's life, he or she is up a creek without a paddle. Unfortunately you don't have to look very far or very deeply to know that this is true. Just look around your neighborhood. In the 1950s most suburban middle-class kids wouldn't have dared to tamper with someone's mailbox. It's a federal crime, and it was unthinkable. But not today. It's a pretty common practice and nobody seems to care much about it one way or another.

When American teenager Michael Fay was going to be caned in Singapore for his acts of vandalism, it produced quite an uproar here in the United States. Not surprising to some, and shocking to others, was the typical American's response: "Cane him!!" We wouldn't think of doing that here, but we were certainly ready to have them do it for us. "Cane him!" some shouted. "Let's put an end to vandalism once and for all." The sad part about this is that we adults seem to lack internal discipline ourselves, thereby setting up our kids to act out, then we let them get away with it or get them off when they get caught, and then we want one of them to be brutally punished by another country so we don't have to be responsible for the brutality.

Wouldn't it be a lot kinder and saner if we'd just raise our kids more thoughtfully? When people act thoughtfully things work out much more smoothly. What if we followed through with some serious consequences for damaging mailboxes? What if our judges followed through with our laws a little more instead of pitying our children quite so much? What if we parents had limits and structure and discipline at home so that our kids could grow up to be happy and productive instead of agitated, angry and miserable? Do we really want our children to be like this? It doesn't have to be this way. Every day, every single day of our lives, it's our choice.

9

Expect Your Child to Fulfill *Your* Dreams

Near-Tragedy in the Career Trenches

A 1998 Louis Harris Poll of college students from the class of 2001 whose parents were employed asked if they would "ever consider" the same career as either parent. A whopping 62 percent said "no." With that in mind, imagine that your son appears to have genuine talent as an artist. He wants to go to art school. You and your relatives, going back two generations at least, are scientists, lawyers and businessmen—professions that are "hard" as opposed to "soft." From the very beginning, you gently mold your son in the direction of one of these careers. You never come out and say that you have strong feelings about his future career choice. You like the artwork that he does in school. You note that he's talented. And you continue to encourage him to develop a wide range of interests and skills as he progresses through school. Because he comes from a bright, successful family he does well in everything he tackles. So far, so good.

In college, your son slowly begins to gravitate toward art and design. He continues to excel in everything he gets his hands on but it is becoming clearer each day that he isn't leaning toward law, science or business. Concerned that he won't be able to survive in the world if he makes art his major field of study, and worried that even if he eventually does, the years of struggle and hardship would never be worth it, you lovingly begin to nudge him toward one of the "harder" professions. You have a good relationship with your son. You have done many things with him along his path to adulthood. He respects your opinion. One day he calls home and tells you that he has begun therapy with one of the psychologists on campus "to help him sort out some things that are causing him a bit of anxiety."

You get a little nervous but don't recognize it as fear. Instead, you hear those inner messages as a call to action. Something or someone may be threatening the well-being of one of your brood. You must act. You call the college counseling center. They tell you that they would rather not even acknowledge that your son is or isn't in counseling without his consent. You rattle your legal saber a bit, being careful not to use up too much of your emotional currency by being unduly intimidating. They don't budge. Exasperated, you call your son back, being careful not to mention that you tried to speak to the counseling center staff. You ask how he's doing. You inquire about the therapy sessions. He says they're going fine. He sounds cheerful but isn't disclosing an excessive amount of information. You say, "Good, I'm glad things are going well," as you end the call and begin strategizing your next move.

So far so good? Not really. In fact, if this is you, we caution you right now that you are already well down a potentially destructive path and that the farther you go down that path from now on, the worse it will get. Our advice? Turn around. Get your bearings. Pack up your knapsack and head toward home. When you get back to that fork in the road, take the other path.

The Other Fork in the Road

Every ten or twenty years somebody funds a major study of twins in an effort to determine the role of genetics in human behavior. Nowadays these studies are more sophisticated than they were originally. They look at identical twins who were raised together, identical twins who were raised apart from each other, fraternal twins raised together or apart, other siblings raised together and apart, and so forth. They then use some pretty clever statistical formulas to pull apart all the different sources of variation among these different groups of people and in the process are able to remove most of the variation due to environmental factors. This leaves scientists with a fair estimate of the heritability of human traits like intelligence and personality.

One of the largest and most recent of these twin studies was conducted at the University of Minnesota and reported in *Science* in 1990. The preliminary results were astonishing. We have known for years that intelligence has a pretty high heritability coefficient so that result wasn't such a big deal next to the spectacular discovery that as much as 43 percent of our career choice and 49 percent of our religious preference are determined by genetics. What's so exciting about these findings is that they are so sensible! Think about how people *really* gravitate toward a career or a way of celebrating their spirituality. If you're left-brained, analytic, logical and linear, wouldn't it make sense that you aren't going to be drawn to the arts or social work? And if you're right-brained, highly intuitive and tend to process things simultaneously and non-linearly, wouldn't it make some sense that you would tend toward the mystical and poetic in your spiritual celebrations?

What does this mean to the average parent? It means that we can begin by choosing the path less traveled when we get to that fork in the road. We can go back and re-read Kahlil Gibran's statement affirming that we do not own our children. We can call up a psychologist and ask for help in modifying our outdated belief that we must mold our children into our image lest they be condemned to a lifetime of frustration and failure. And then we can celebrate, along with the choirs of very relieved angels singing in the heavens, that there may be an artist in the family for the first time since the 1700s.

Perhaps it would help if we describe this other path a little more. Taking this path means that parents have to be more grown up than they used to be. It takes more emotional depth for a parent to take this path, and it takes more faith. We are not suggesting that the path you should take is one of neglect. If your son has absolutely no artistic talent whatsoever but has been encouraged by a misguided instructor along the way, by all means, talk with your son. Point out your concerns. Be tactful, gracious, but direct. That's just fine.

Caring Without Arrogance

We recognize that most parents don't mean to be arrogant when they push their children toward a career, but in most cases it is an arrogant mistake to make nonetheless. Just to confuse you, we'll add that there are times when it isn't arrogant, and when it is very necessary. Remember that "in the old days" career choices were severely limited. Your parents operated a farm. This was how you all survived. It was literally a matter of life and death. So you learned to operate a farm, and therefore you survived. Your father was a shoemaker. You weren't much more than serfs. It was 1200 A.D. There was no room for you to maneuver. You became a shoemaker, or nothing at all. And so you survived.

Times have changed and along with the changes have come an infinite array of choices and the freedom that accompanies them. But unlimited choice produces increased anxiety—in both parents and children. If I'm not going to be a farmer, what am I going to be? If I don't like making shoes, what will I do to make a living and support my family? These are the questions that will face nearly every Western industrialized family in the twenty-first century.

How can we be caring without being arrogant? How do we help our kids get from childhood into adulthood with a clear identity in place? It's not as hard as you might think, actually. But for some it will first require a major shift in attitude and belief. The good news is that human development has some universals to it. All children must accomplish certain developmental tasks regardless of what culture they grow up in. Our first bit of advice is that you find a stage theory, such as Erik Erikson's, that is based on these cross-cultural universals, and then learn it, study it, learn some more, memorize it, study it again, research it and then do it all again, until you know it inside and out.

While that may seem tedious and time-consuming, we can assure you that it will save you thousands of hours of heartache and confusion as you raise your children. A set of stages like Erikson's is particularly useful because it gives us plenty of room to work out individual solutions to life's problems rather than saying there is only one right way to grow up. It also helps us troubleshoot where we are stuck in life. For example, during the identity formation stage— from about age fifteen through twenty-eight—our job is to clarify who we are and what we want to be, how we want to live, what we like and don't like, whom we like and don't like, and what we will believe, among others. It is also our job to leave home and go out into the world, paying our own way and building our own support system. Once you know this, it is fairly easy to diagnose problems. If your twenty-five-year-old son still lives at home, pays no rent and still lives like a high school kid, then the two of you have a problem. If your two-year-old daughter is afraid to leave your side, clings like a vine and never says "no," then take a look. If your eighteen-year-old hasn't questioned anything he learned as a child, or that he was taught to believe as a child, he may be getting stuck.

Whenever we say things like that at lectures or seminars, there is always the inevitable debate with someone who takes exception to what we say about identity formation; but in nearly every case, the person's defensiveness seems to stem from the fear that there might be something wrong with his or her child or parenting efforts. As much as we can understand some parents' discomfort with this, we have a hard time thinking of many cases in which it is healthy for a twenty-five-year-old to still be living at home.

With the above considerations in mind, here are some pointers that have been used successfully by competent parents we have known throughout the years.

Examples of Raising Whole, Competent Children

The Art and Design Major

Your son appears to have genuine talent as an artist. He does well in everything all the way through school because he is bright like you. You have watched the transformation that takes place in his face when he is engaged in, thinking about or otherwise wrapped up in artistic pursuits. Your heart warms at the thought of his discovering what he's meant to be in life. What excites you most isn't that there will be an artist in the family. What excites you most is that your son seems to have locked onto his target—the one determined by his genes and his childhood experiences. The thrill of watching him pursue his dreams is immediate for you because you've done the same thing—you know what it's like to go after something so tentative but ultimately so engaging and correct. You've experienced the excitement of finding your own identity.

As he approaches his junior year in college, he finds himself walking into the academic advising office on his college campus and changing his major to art and design. He's excited and a little anxious. Change is always a little unnerving and you can never be perfectly certain how loved ones will respond to your decisions. He asks himself a series of rapid-fire questions: "Am I being impulsive? Am I avoiding something? Am I just taking the easy way out? Can I really make a living doing this? How will I fit into my family structure when everyone else is into more traditional 'hard' pursuits? What if I find out five years from now that I've made the wrong decision and make another mid-course correction? Will everyone think I'm crazy?" These are wonderful questions for someone to ask himself. This is what makes life so marvelous, mysterious, engaging and worthwhile. When a kid asks these questions, he is doing his identity work.

A college student is perfectly able to find the answers to these questions. But only if his family can support him through thick and thin. Think of the message we give our college kids when we say, "We see you are struggling with what to do when you grow up. We like that about you. We know you will find what you're looking for. We can't do it for you. Remember that you don't have to do life perfectly and that the only way to find your true path is to make mistakes. If there's any reasonable way we can help, let us know. Otherwise, go for it!" The message is: "We are excited to see you growing up. We know you can do it. Struggle is good. You are competent. It's good to take calculated risks. We will love you no matter what happens. We like to see you grapple with life. It's good for the soul."

The Tuba Player

You have "that talk" with your elementary school daughter. You know, the one about playing a musical instrument. She thinks about it, and then says she'll talk it over with the music teacher. A few days later, she comes home and announces that she wants to play a musical instrument.

"What have you chosen, honey?" you ask.

"The tuba!" she exclaims. "It's so cool! I've always thought the tuba was cool! My teacher said they needed a tuba player, too!" You have nothing against the tuba whatsoever. Without the tuba, the band or orchestra would lack beat and drive, you say to yourself. Another part of you is whispering, "I was hoping she'd pick the violin or piano." You decide to play it low-key and go along with her decision and tell her that it's a fine decision. You discover that it's still nagging at you two days later.

But you are a good parent, and you know that you must let your daughter discover what works best for her. You discuss it with your husband. You both agree that two things could result. She could either take to the tuba and run with it enthusiastically right through middle school and high school and on into college; or she could lose her interest after a year or two and decide to give it up. Let's say the latter happens. What should you do? Well, if your daughter has established a pattern of starting things and then dropping them after a few weeks, you ought to intervene and require her to follow through at least to the end of the school year. Why? So she learns that decisions have consequences, that commitments mean something, and so that she will weigh her decisions more carefully in the future.

If your daughter does not have a pattern of backing out of commitments then let her drop out after a year or two. What will be gained by this? Will she still have learned anything along the way? Of course she will have learned something along the way. She will have learned how to read music. She will have learned how an orchestra or band functions. She will have learned how to work as part of a team. And she will have learned that after some reflection it is okay to change your mind, and that you won't be ostracized or criticized for doing so. See? Even if she drops out after a year or two, she won't have lost anything, and she will have gained much. That's life. That's how we learn about life. And that's good parenting in action.

There are a lot of happy tuba players out there. You can see them in symphony orchestras and bands all around the world. You can see the happy smiles on their faces, the glow of accomplishment that surrounds them, and the obvious satisfaction in their eyes. They are doing what moves their souls.

The Entrepreneur

Your seventeen-year-old knows that he is expected to get a summer job to help pay for his car insurance, gasoline, a small portion of his clothes and incidentals. Last summer, he worked for an office-cleaning outfit at minimum wage, and he really worked hard. But he hated it, so he and a couple of his friends put together a plan to market themselves as a yard clean-up, odd job, house repair company for the summer. When you were a kid, you worked at the same factory for the last three years of high school and for the first three years of college, working your way into a better position during the last two years with the company. After college you actually contacted this company and applied for a management position, which you were offered immediately because of your long work history there. You have worked there very successfully all of your life. In fact, you're the new CEO.

As a father, you may or may not have some ambivalence about your son's plans to start his own business. On the one hand, you may fully appreciate the importance of this kind of entrepreneurship in youth. It shows ambition, drive and a willingness to take risks. On the other hand, your own career path with its steady and reliable commitment to one company, as well as the predictable, consistent paychecks that come with a salaried position may be crowding out that other viewpoint. Indeed, you may secretly worry that the guys will encounter some unforeseen resistance in their marketing efforts causing them to abandon their business plan altogether and ending up with no summer jobs at all. This could be a financial disaster and could result in terrible heartache and emotional distress in your household. These issues are rarely clear-cut.

What do you do? If your teenager has a long history of starting things and dropping them soon afterwards, then by all means tell him that he hasn't earned the right to be an entrepreneur. Kids who haven't been baptized by fire, who haven't paid their dues for at least one summer of forty-hour-a-week employment, probably should do so. They should probably get a regular job if the likelihood of their following through with self-employment is low. But this isn't the case for all kids. In our opinion, there isn't a huge risk in letting your teenager try this out for a summer. In the worst-case scenario, he and his friends will break their backs trying to make the business go and will discover that it's a lot harder than they ever anticipated. When wise kids see the handwriting on the wall, they often try to keep the one business going while taking a part-time job, if only at minimum wage, so that they don't come up empty-handed at the end of the summer.

Yes, it's a risk. But we wonder how many tremendously successful business men and women would never have tried to start their companies had they not been supported and guided by their families during adolescence. Our kids need to find out what they are cut out to do. It takes a certain personality type to be an entrepreneur. Sometimes people envision being self-employed because they've had a bad experience with a superior and "never want to work for someone else again," when in fact they aren't cut out for self-employment. They simply need to figure out how to deal with poor management and then continue working within the corporate world. But others really do thrive in a largely self-motivated world, and we would all be worse off were it not for them. Before you try to squash your teenager's enthusiasm for starting a small business ask yourself honestly and courageously if you are getting in your child's way, and your own.

The Agnostic

If you haven't felt challenged by this chapter yet, try this one on for size. What do you do when your thirteen-year-old comes home from confirmation class and says, "I really like the pastor who's teaching the class and I like doing stuff with the other kids, but to be honest, I don't know if I believe much of this stuff in the Bible. I understand that it may not be literal, either. But I'm even questioning if there's actually a God or not." You can see the sincerity in her eyes and you can hear it in her voice. Your mind starts scanning through its high-speed memory banks and logical folders looking for an appropriate interpretation of your child's statement and for a response that won't blow up in either of your faces. You notice your heart speeds up and your breathing stops for a second.

"Hm-m-m," you respond in the most neutral but interested tone of voice that you can muster. And then the answer dawns on you, and you feel yourself breathe a sigh of relief. Thank goodness for Erik Erikson, you say to yourself just before you continue with a truly helpful reply: "I'm really pleased to hear that you're struggling with this stuff. That's what you're supposed to do at this age. I'm proud of you." It just barely shows in a flicker of recognition that sweeps across your child's face but what she's thinking to herself is: "Wow! Does that ever feel good to hear!" There is a moment of comfortable silence and then she deftly steers the conversation in a new direction: "By the way, Mom, what do you think about the bill Congress is considering for that proposed manned mission to Mars? We had a debate about it in class today and I'm not sure on which side of the argument I'll eventually land." You smile warmly and say to yourself, "We *have* done a pretty good job of raising her. Thank you for your help, God."

Give It Up

We were watching some political interview program on television one evening when we heard a very well-educated man on the panel say that he was upset because many people were trying to degrade our former presidents. When asked by the interviewer what he meant, the man said that he was referring to the "lie" that has been spread that Dwight Eisenhower had a long-standing affair with his female driver during World War II. The man went on to explain that people were doing this to try to justify some of the seamier behavior of contemporary politicians. Granted, there is some pretty questionable behavior among contemporary politicians, but does that give us license to distort historical fact? After all, Dwight Eisenhower *did* have a long-standing affair with his driver during World War II. It's a historical fact.

Growing up is hard to do, in part because it requires that

we take off our blinders and eventually let people off of the pedestals on which we have placed them. The Holocaust did happen despite what some racist hate-mongers would like us to believe. Stanley Milgram's research on obedience to authority suggests that it could happen anywhere, including here. History shows that it has happened all over the globe, the "Killing Fields" of Cambodia being a more recent example. People who live by high moral standards don't have to worry about their children being unduly influenced by others, they don't have to fabricate history in order to support their morality, and they don't have to spout and brag and advertise their high moral standards. All they have to do is live a moral life. It really is that simple. If you counter one man's lies with your own lies, what have you accomplished? People will just think that you're dishonest or naive.

We remember some stunning research that was done a couple of decades ago. The investigators looked not only at parents' values but also at how much they actually lived according to those values. Then they interviewed their college-aged children regarding their feelings about their parents. Regardless of whether their parents were liberal or conservative, religious or atheist, hawk or dove, if these parents lived according to their own values and *did things* that showed commitment, then these children had great respect for their parents. If these parents just paid lip service to their values and if their actions were inconsistent with their values, then their children did not have much respect for them. Even more importantly, children from the value-consistent families grew up to have clear values and identities themselves; whereas the children from the "lip-service families" grew up to be confused and unclear about their own values. Some of them even stated it bluntly: "My parents were phonies."

These are harsh words, indeed. But sometimes harsh is necessary. It is hypocritical to tell our children that we want them to grow up to be strong, clear, consistent, thoughtful, committed adults when we aren't that way ourselves, and when we aren't willing to give our kids clear messages to that effect. Children *do* learn what they live. It is sad to see otherwise well-meaning parents clinging to their adolescents for dear life, terrified that if they let go a little more they will ruin their kids. It is sad because just the opposite is true. Teens will make it into successful adulthood if they do a lot of the struggling on their own. Parents who are able to gradually let go of their kids as they near their twenties send kids a clear message that it is good to grow up.

One of the wisest pieces of counsel that we can pass along to our clients as their children approach adulthood is, *"Give it up."* This doesn't mean that you should neglect your teenagers. They need to have a curfew, chores and accountability. But a lot of letting go has to happen on the parents' part, and it isn't always easy, which is why we give that advice from time to time. If you believe that your children are your property, then this chapter is for you.

Being a parent today requires a lot more flexibility than ever before. The challenge is to provide enough structure and guidance so that our kids grow up with internal rudders but not so much structure that they can't grow up at all. It's quite a challenge. Challenge is good. It keeps us alive.

Part III
Go for It

10

If Rats Can Do It, So Can You

Priorities, Priorities, Priorities

In this chapter, we challenge you. Over the past decade there has been a proliferation of books and tapes designed to help us attain higher states of consciousness, nirvana and bliss. Because so many of us are working on this part of ourselves, we would like to remind everyone that building a house on slushy, wet, sandy ground in an absolutely fabulous setting can be very different from building one on bedrock, even in an unexciting location. The Three Little Pigs can tell you more about this if you don't quite get the picture.

139

It is disturbing to see otherwise well-educated, intelligent people focusing on all of these grand schemes for attaining bliss, nirvana and permanently altered states of consciousness while their children run amok: These kids are boundary-less, rudderless, empty and essentially parent-less. It's not that trying to attain bliss is wrong. It's just that trying to attain bliss when you don't have the basics of your home and family in order means your priorities have gotten off-track.

We especially appreciate books like Mary Pipher's *The Shelter of Each Other: Rebuilding Our Families,* and William Doherty's *The Intentional Family: How to Build Family Ties in Our Modern World.* These practicing psychologists have bravely taken on the most mundane, and therefore spiritual, of causes by writing books that implore us to take the day-to-day stuff seriously again. And we need to do that. When our children can log onto the Internet and play sixty-four-bit video games against opponents in Outer Mongolia who are connected via satellite uplink, but can't sustain a pleasant conversation with family or friends that includes eye contact and appropriate gestures and facial expressions, something is wrong. When our children know how much a Jeep Grand Cherokee costs but haven't a clue as to how to run a washer or dryer or fry an egg or take care of a pet consistently enough so that it doesn't die of dehydration or starvation, something is wrong. And perhaps most of all, when it is *de rigueur* for children to hold their parents hostage by whining, pouting, tantrums, bargaining and other manipulations, then it's time for a change.

But a change to what? We hear parents asking, "How can

I get my child to pick up after herself? How can I get my child to stop throwing tantrums? How can I get my twenty-six-year-old to move out on his own? How can I . . . ?" If only parents started to ask this question: "How can I create some internal discipline in myself so that my children can learn internal discipline by being around me?" To be a competent parent, or not to be a competent parent. That is the question.

At the Checkout Counter

Your four-year-old whines, screws up his face in tortured contortions, grimaces, stamps his feet and punches you with a limp fist when you tell him "no," he can't buy any candy at the checkout counter. This has become such a terrible problem for you that you dread going shopping. You fantasize leaving him in the car, but that would be neglectful. You dream about running away to a remote tropical island, leaving your children to be raised by your husband or mother until they are past their teen years and well out of the nest. In the past, you tried ignoring him, but the tantrums always escalate and become so intense that you are afraid he'll hurt himself somehow. He might turn blue and pass out. *You*, on the other hand, are so embarrassed that you first turn bright crimson and then all the blood rushes out of your head as you turn a whiter shade of pale. It's not a pretty sight. And it's destroying your child.

What can you do? If you go back to your general psychology textbook from high school or your freshman year of college, you will find some very fascinating work by the occasionally maligned B. F. Skinner, whose brilliant work permanently revolutionized psychology. He put a rat into what is now known as a Skinner Box—a box with a lever and a food dispenser on one wall—and then guess what happened? That's right. Because rats are naturally curious and because they naturally get up on their haunches and poke around with their little paws, the rat accidentally, but eventually, pressed the lever; and lo and behold, a food pellet was dispensed and the hungry rat got his first taste of the exciting world of cause and effect.

Hang in there for a moment. The good part's coming. Next, Skinner spent a decade or two researching all the ins and outs of this operant conditioning as he called it. He quickly found that if the rat had to press the lever several times before it got rewarded—if it had to work for its food—then its lever-pressing behavior would be much stronger and much less resistant to extinction. Furthermore, if the reward came at irregular intervals, like the payoffs from a slot machine, the behavior was the strongest of all.

Now here comes the really good part. One of the most useful contributions from operant conditioning research is how you go about getting rid of behavior you don't want anymore. There are several ways to extinguish behavior, but by far the most effective, humane and decent way to do it is to simply stop reinforcing it. So when Skinner turned off the power to the food dispenser the rats eventually figured out that there was no point in pressing the lever because it wouldn't produce any food—cause and effect again. If the slot machine you're playing never, ever, ever paid anything at all again, you'd eventually stop playing it.

Of course, this extinction doesn't happen all at once. What happens is that the rat goes through an extinction burst at first. This is a flurry of frantic lever-pulling the likes of which you've never seen. Then, gradually, the behavior begins to decrease. But not without a few bursts along the way, as if the rat were thinking to himself, "It's been two days. Maybe that lazy psychologist has repaired this crazy machine by now." Sound familiar? Like a broken vending machine that keeps taking your money?

Here's the other crucial part. If at any time during this gradual extinction process, you reinforce that rat for pulling the lever even once, its rate of lever-pulling behavior increases dramatically, often to levels stronger than before! It's the darnedest thing. Figures 10.1 and 10.2 illustrate this. Study these graphs. Memorize them. Burn them into your brain. They contain some of the most important information a parent can acquire.

FIGURES 10.1

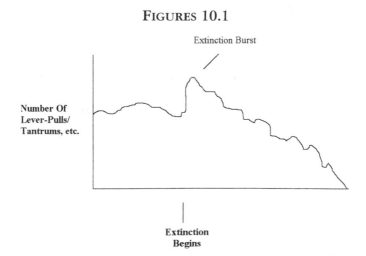

FIGURES 10.2

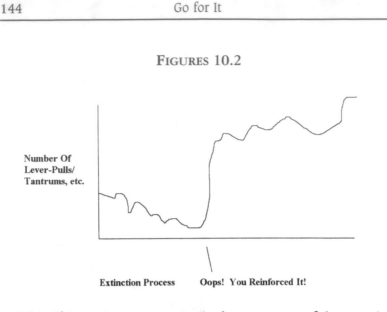

Number Of
Lever-Pulls/
Tantrums, etc.

Extinction Process   Oops! You Reinforced It!

This Skinnerian concept is the key to successful parenting in hundreds of problem situations. Why do we say that? Because in our experience, parents have the most trouble when it comes to setting limits with children, and this is the most effective and humane way to do it. All parents are capable of using this method, but some aren't willing to or don't understand how well this works.

Eliminating Inappropriate Behavior

You may be sitting there reading this chapter and thinking to yourself, "I've tried this extinction procedure, but it doesn't work!" This extinction procedure does work. It really does. But it takes some practice, some coaching and follow-through. To facilitate your use of these procedures, let us outline some of the typical mistakes that we all make when trying to eliminate inappropriate behavior in our kids.

1. If You're Going to Do It, Then Do It: Don't Vacillate

You say "no" to your child, your child starts to throw a fit, then you fuse with your child rather than remaining a separate, distinct person. You sink into the morass of whining and bargaining created by your child. Your guilt escalates. You begin to feel embarrassed. As your anxiety heightens, so do your impotent attempts to control the situation. Instead of maintaining your power by surrendering, being still and calmly resolute, and letting things take their natural extinction course, you choose the typical but tragic error of presuming that if you keep trying you will eventually find the active key to end this misery. But you never do. You never will. There are no actions to take short of abusing your child, and you don't want to do that. We've all seen that in grocery stores. It's a painful spectacle that no one wants to take part in or see. So once you decide you're going to ignore the tantrum—once you've started down that path—you are committed. Don't ever lose sight of that.

2. Follow Through 'Til the Very End, and Then Follow Through Some More

This may sound odd, but many people work at this for months until they have achieved remarkable success with their children in the grocery store and then they blow it. Lao-tzu, the Chinese philosopher-poet credited with creating the basic text of Taoism, wrote, "Most people fail when they are on the verge of success, so give as much care to the end as to the beginning, then there will be no failure." We have had this quote attached to the wall of our home and our office for over twenty years and it has served us faithfully and well. B. F. Skinner's research on extinguishing operant behaviors is so clear and unequivocal. Once you remove the reinforcement for a behavior, you must keep it removed. There are no ifs, ands, buts, exceptions, special occasions or soothings of our neurotic consciences. "No" means "no."

What sometimes happens is that after a couple of successful weeks, many of us tend to backslide, as if to say, "This extinction stuff really works. It's been three weeks and my daughter hasn't had one tantrum! She's been so good! I feel a little guilty about all the struggling she's had to do. Maybe I'll buy her some candy at the checkout counter!" If you feel like doing this, please stop yourself and remember that it would be both cruel and confusing to her to do it.

3. Do Not, We Repeat, Do Not Try to Reason with a Child Who Is out of Control

You may think that reasoning with someone who is out of control is a good idea. It isn't a good idea to do this with an adult, and it is silly to do it with a child who is out of control. Watch what happens when other parents try it. Ask someone who is outside of your family to give you an objective, unbiased, painfully honest assessment of you and your child when you try to do it. Brace yourself. It isn't always a comfortable experience to get objective feedback. We're not sure where this extreme stance (as opposed to a balanced one) about reasoning with little kids came from, but this notion of sitting down and reasoning with a child, which is a good idea in some very specific situations, has been blown far out of proportion.

Dealing with the tantrum is really quite simple. Ignore the screaming child on the floor next to you. Smile calmly and with graceful embarrassment at the people staring at you. Say quietly and firmly, "We're learning an important lesson today. Pardon us for the noise." People are very understanding and very appreciative of healthy parents. They will love you for it. Their eyes will glow with warm support. Their energy will lift your spirits. We've seen this happen more than once. It's truly a moment of grace.

4. Whatever You Do, Don't Sabotage Your Spouse

There are all kinds of reasons that people fail themselves and their children when trying to extinguish inappropriate behavior. The last one we will mention here is both serious and obvious to people outside the "parental unit." It occurs when one parent sabotages the other during the extinction process. It is seldom ever done consciously and it almost always happens because of predictable, inherent differences between partners. And it is essential to stop. Couples who do not present a united front to their children not only risk confusing their children, but they also risk damaging their marriages. One parent becomes the good guy and the other becomes the bad guy. The kids clearly gravitate toward one over the other. Before you know it, the couple is in divorce court. If Dad says "no candy" at the grocery store and Mom gives in all the time, look out. They're in for trouble.

What Else Do You Have to Learn?

Applying operant conditioning principles in practical, everyday situations was originally called behavior modification. You may remember that term. Good old behavior modification was taught to every up-and-coming school-teacher and millions of young parents back in the 1960s and 1970s. It also worked. But like so much other technology created by we Americans, it was overused, misused, beaten to death, eventually misunderstood and then discarded. Sort of. Part of why it lost favor for a while is that fads come and go in this country. So for those of you who weren't around in the early 1970s and for those of you who were but can't remember, here are a few additional elements of behavior modification that might be helpful.

Define Behaviors Clearly

When you say, "I want to stop my son from being rude," you're headed for trouble because "rude" is such a nebulous term that it won't be clear whether you should reward something, extinguish it or what. And your son will argue you into the corner about your imprecision and will be correct in doing so. But if you say, "The behavior I want my son to stop is saying the three worst swear words that he says," then you're in good shape. Because once you define the behavior clearly, you will be much less likely to give up.

The general rule of thumb is that if you ask a group of strangers to count how many times the behavior occurred in a day, they all ought to pretty much agree with each other and with you. But if you say you saw five incidents of rudeness and one of the strangers says he saw one, and another says she saw ten, and another says twenty, then obviously the behavior isn't defined clearly enough. When you tell the therapist that your daughter has tantrums in the grocery store, we certainly hope that she or he asks you what you mean by a tantrum. One parent answered our query by saying, "Tantrum. You know. A tantrum. She rolls her eyes, sighs and walks over and stands by the exit until I've paid for the groceries and am ready to leave." That may indeed be a passive-aggressive tantrum, but it is certainly different than if she were to fall to the floor screaming and turning blue because she's holding her breath. Details are important sometimes.

Count the Behavior for a Few Days Before You Start Changing Anything

This is crucial for two reasons. First, you need to know how much of a problem you have so you can see whether your son is making progress or not. Second, you need to know if it's really a problem worth modifying. One of the frequent and delightful outcomes of getting this baseline measure of behavior is the discovery that you really don't have a problem after all. Your son actually doesn't swear much anymore. He used to swear, but that gradually changed quite a while ago, and your impression of him hasn't kept pace. This is quite common.

Find a Reward That Is Truly Rewarding to Your Child

Okay, parents, this is where you have to acknowledge that your child is not one of your appendages. A reward is defined as something that your child is willing to work for, not what you think your child will be willing to work for. If your child isn't willing to work for money because it has no meaning for her at age five, then don't use it as a reward. If your child hates going to movies, then don't say, "You can earn the right to go to the movies if you reduce the number of swear words to three per week."

We know this sounds pretty obvious, but often when people set up a behavior modification program they do the darnedest things at first—like using rewards that are absolutely meaningless to their child and then getting angry at the child for not responding to the program. When a behavior modification program isn't working, it's the responsibility of the parents to figure out what they didn't set up properly in the first place. That's what behavior modification means.

Use Punishment Very Sparingly, and Before You Do, Ask Yourself If You're Needing to Do It Because You Aren't Paying Enough Attention to Your Child

Many parents don't spend enough time with their children anymore. Oh, they may be in the same room, or in the same car, rushing from one hyped activity to the next. But does that really constitute paying attention? One of the greatest little pieces of research we ever read in the psychology journals was a behavioral analysis of the time and energy that it takes to go out of your way to compliment children before they make a mistake, contrasted with the time and energy it takes to correct ignored children after they have made a mistake. If your children have been playing quietly upstairs on a rainy day for over an hour you can:

1. Stop what you're doing for two minutes (120 tiny little seconds), bound up the stairs, walk casually past their room, poke your head in the door and say, cheerfully, "I am really impressed! You kids are playing so nicely. Thanks very much."

2. Wait a few more minutes while you put what you think are the finishing touches on that report that's due tomorrow, until the kids have finally had enough of the rainy day, the confinement and each other, at which time they will . . . well, you know.

It's *so* simple. But it is human to often ignore things until a crisis hits. This indicates to us, anyway, that too many people simply don't have the time or make the time to raise children anymore. It is your job to create the atmosphere in your home.

If You Try to Change More Than One or Two Behaviors at a Time, Go Directly to Jail

This is a direct violation of the principle that small changes yield big results. We have grown children. We know how rewarding and how hard it is to raise kids. We know that when children are way out of control, it is often the parents' fantasy to have a magic wand and change twenty things all at once in their children. But life doesn't work that way, and it's lucky that it doesn't. As Stanislaus Leszcynski, king of Poland, wrote in 1763, "It is happy for human nature that there are desires which cannot be satisfied. Otherwise, the most sorry man would make himself master of the world."

The simple reality is that parents who have a few rules and enforce them consistently make the best parents, at least when it comes to discipline. Discipline is supposed to teach something, not kill a child's spirit. It's supposed to help children have basic respect for parents, and for them to learn about structure and limits, not to give parents absolute, totalitarian dominion over their children. Behavior modification is not a tool to help parents become even more abusive or neglectful than they are. It's supposed to be used with discretion, wisdom, care and love.

11

The Best Things About Parents Who Choose to Grow: A Typical Success Story

If you have read this far in the present book, you may be wondering how likely it is for parents to change once they've been on a particular parenting path for many years. After all, negotiating *the straits of parenthood* is a big job for everyone but especially for today's overworked, overextended parents. In fact, people who *choose* to change *will* change. What's more, it is really true that no matter how old you are, if you begin to make a change today, it will positively impact each of your family members all the way down the intergenerational line. We have worked with people in their seventies and eighties who decided that it was finally time to clear things up for themselves and with their loved ones, and we can assure you that the changes they made created positive outcomes throughout their families.

Eric, Pamela and Bobby Jamison

In chapter 1, we briefly introduced the Jamison family. If you recall, they had approached us with a basic question about their five-year-old son, Bobby. They subsequently made an appointment for family therapy during which time it became clear that they had a bigger problem on their hands than they had initially let on. Bobby was having an average of four major tantrums a day, bedtime was a nightmare, and simple tasks like brushing teeth had turned into huge battles that Bobby always won. In fact, Eric was beside himself to the point of contemplating moving out for fear of what he might do if he remained in the house. The system had gotten out of control.

You may also recall that we began by telling them that we admired their desire to work through the problem and that they obviously loved their son. We then framed the problem as resulting from their specific methods not working for them, rather than their goals being faulty. Their goals were fine, but too vague.

Given all that you know about child development either from reading books or simply observing people throughout your own lifetime, we would ask you at this point to imagine what Bobby might be like when he is thirteen, eighteen, twenty-three and perhaps thirty if Eric and Pamela continue to raise him exactly the way they are now doing. Will he have trouble with impulse control? Will he have problems relating to other people? What will happen when he is given a particularly challenging term-paper assignment when he is a freshman in high school? What kind of friend will he grow up to be? What kind of marital partner might he make? Also, what kind of marriage will Eric and Pamela have five years from now when Bobby is ten. Once you've done that, continue to read this chapter and in the following pages we will share with you the outcome of this very fine family's work.

Family Patterns

We explained to the Jamisons that they were in a very good position because of Bobby's age: The younger the child, the easier it is to make mid-course corrections. With the bulk of our clients, our initial evaluation sessions include some time for us to map out their genograms on the flipchart in our office. This can be especially helpful when working with couples because it gives each partner a much clearer idea of where the other came from and how his or her "hot buttons" were installed. A genogram is like a family tree, but in this case the focus is on behavioral patterns, conscious and unconscious messages, themes, physical and emotional health issues, and so forth. When we are done doing their genograms, we and the parents usually have a much better idea of where their problems are coming from.

What we discovered is that Eric came from a family

in which open conflict was frowned upon. This occurred
indirectly, because conflict never seemed to actually occur.
We asked Eric how his parents resolved conflicts and his
first response was that he couldn't recall them ever having
many conflicts. As we explored his family dynamics further
Eric was finally able to see that *everyone* has conflicts, including his parents. Then he asked himself, "How *did* they
resolve their conflicts, and what did I learn as a result?"
What he learned was that his father simply deferred to his
mother whenever they had differences. "Aha!" he exclaimed.
"I think I'm beginning to get the picture. I'm *afraid* of having conflict and my way of diverting it is to defer to Pamela
all the time!" He was excited about his new insight and so
was Pamela.

Pamela already knew that she came from a family with
more obvious troubles. Her mother was moody and inconsistent and leaned on Pamela too much for help around the
house and for emotional support. Her father dealt with his
wife by busying himself so much at work and with chores,
errands and community volunteer work that he was seldom
home. But he was a good provider and was honored in the
community for his kindness and willingness to help, so of
course it was very hard for Pamela to recognize that he had
unwittingly abandoned her to Mom and, indirectly,
had used her as a shield. The upshot of all this was that
she had made an unconscious vow as a little girl that when
she grew up she would make sure that *her* children would be
able to enjoy their childhoods.

You probably get the drift of it now. Pamela began parenthood with an unhealed wound about being overworked,

unsupported, emotionally abandoned and missing out on much of the safety and fun of childhood. She ended up indulging Bobby and being way too permissive with him in her attempts to move beyond her own childhood shortages. What she needed was a strong partner who could have loving conflict with her and thereby help her find the balance for which she unknowingly longed. Eric began parenthood with an unhealed wound about fear of standing up for himself in close relationships and about expressing anger in general. Like his father before him, Eric chose to minimize conflict by deferring to Pamela and by so doing actually let her down by letting her operate out of her woundedness even though he knew it wasn't good for her, him or Bobby. In other words, he was partially reenacting not only his own childhood but also Pamela's—the Dad who isn't there much.

Some people believe that once they have uncovered these patterns their work is done and then they wonder why nothing has gotten better. Doing this sort of work is not an end in itself. It is simply one of the stepping stones along the path. It can be a very helpful one, though. If either Eric or Pamela have difficulty following through with a program of change for Bobby, it will be useful to know where they are most likely getting stuck. Having these patterns identified from the beginning makes troubleshooting a behavior change program a lot easier.

The Program

The next step in their process was for Eric and Pamela to set up their initial behavioral program for Bobby. In keeping with the principles of behavior modification discussed in chapter 10, we asked them to begin with *one* behavior. At first they balked at this idea. The whole system was out of control and if they didn't get some drastic changes fast, there was no telling what might happen, they said. We explained again why they could expect more success by starting with one behavior, and then we asked them to have some faith that this might work. What did they have to lose, we asked them. They agreed, and selected bedtime compliance as their first goal.

First, the Jamisons defined what compliance and noncompliance would mean. The goal was to have Bobby in his bedroom, with the door shut, and "reasonably quiet," by 8:00 P.M. every night. Noncompliance included Bobby saying "no," having a tantrum, going to bed and then appearing in the family room a few minutes later asking for a drink of water or a bedtime story, or being in his room with the door shut but screaming or crying or having a tantrum. They decided that it was okay if Bobby was singing, talking to himself or humming, as long as he was in his room with the door shut. Early on, Pamela asked if it would be harmful if Bobby cried himself to sleep laying by the closed door of his bedroom. She could feel the ghosts of her childhood whispering to her. We explained that we knew of no child who was damaged by falling asleep on the floor by his door a few nights and that once he figured out that the maneuver wasn't going to work, he'd decide to sleep in his bed, which was, after all, much more comfortable. She acknowledged courageously that this was going to be hard for her, and Eric put his hand on hers and complimented her for her courage as she shed a few tears.

Next they did seven days of behavioral recording to get a baseline with which to compare the impact of their program. As rigid or as compulsive as this may seem, remember that we are dealing with a system that is out of control, and so stepping back to see exactly how bad the problem is, is a very useful thing to do. They admitted that it was hard to be patient and just record behavior when they knew what they wanted to do was jump right in and start changing things. But they did the recording, and they did it well. When they returned with their baseline data the first thing they both said was that they were amazed at the extent of the problem and that the recording process had already helped them be more objective and detached. They also noticed that it helped them to be more concerned about how Bobby's behavior was harmful for *Bobby* than about how it was stressing *them*. This realization allowed them to be even more objective and resolute in their desire to follow through with the change program. Things were looking up, they said.

And then came the actual change program. We helped Eric and Pamela understand that feelings of guilt, pity, fear and sadness for and about Bobby, mixed with anger at him, themselves and us, would be normal during the first few days, and that to expect anything else would be unrealistic and unfair to themselves. We also reminded them to let themselves depend on as much support as they could find at this time because they would need it to counteract their strong urges to sabotage the program. They returned to report on how it was going. Pamela burst into tears and then

Eric's lip quivered and he "got all choked up." It was *so* hard, she said. It brought up so many old feelings for her. She wasn't sure she could follow through. Eric took a huge risk and said that he was angry at the possibility that Pamela might not be able to follow through. He also said he loved her and would keep supporting her no matter what happened.

As we discussed their efforts thus far, what emerged was that they were much more successful than they had imagined. The first night was predictably difficult. Bobby screamed and cried and raged and manipulated and tried every trick in the book to stay up later. But they made it through, and indeed, Bobby had fallen asleep next to his closed door as the Jamisons lay awake fantasizing that they had caused irreparable harm to their son. The next morning, they acted as if nothing had happened and made a special effort to be as positive and upbeat as they could without appearing artificial. Bobby seemed fine. The next night, Bobby had another tantrum and tried several tricks in the book, but not all of them. The Jamisons recorded all of his behaviors as per the program they had set up, so as they looked at their data with us they suddenly realized that things were actually better by the second night. We complimented them for the work they had done thus far and managed to mention in mid-sentence somewhere that they were now in the process of reprogramming the unhealthy software that had been installed in them when they were kids. They both glowed despite their intermittent fear that they were hurting Bobby and that they might not be able to keep at it.

Working Through the Problems

The next three nights yielded steady progress. Eric and Pamela and Bobby were succeeding. Eric and Pamela's ambivalence continued, too. Part of them was proud of themselves and of Bobby for the changes they were making, and another part felt guilty and sad. They found themselves feeling sorry for Bobby as he "dutifully said goodnight," and they both felt bad that he was in his bed, alone, in the dark, while they were quietly enjoying some much-needed time together. They felt selfish and asked themselves if this was what good parenting was all about. Pamela asked Eric, "Isn't Bobby going to feel abandoned by us because of this? It seems so cruel just to say 'goodnight' after his bedtime story, shut his door, and then come back downstairs and watch TV and spend time alone. Maybe we should go back up and tuck him in a second time." For a split-second she could feel herself as a little girl back in her own room, tired and lonely, wondering if anyone in her family cared at all about her.

Eric was also confused. He found himself relieved that Bobby was quietly settled in for the night, but he could see the pain on his wife's face and his heart went out to her. After battling with these two feelings for a moment, Eric heard himself say, "Oh, I suppose it wouldn't hurt. After all, he *has* been so good." As his words entered the room he also felt himself recoiling in shock at what he had just said, but it was too late, he told himself. Pamela looked so relieved that Eric didn't dare take it back. *That* would have broken his heart. So up they went. On the outside they were giggling and smiling but on the inside they were both faintly aware of feeling guilty and ashamed for giving into the urge they knew wasn't good for them or Bobby.

They opened the door and the light from the hallway framed Bobby's face. He looked up, sleepy and puzzled at first, and asked, "What?" Their mutual ambivalence heightened as they looked at each other. "Uh . . ." Pamela said. "Uh," Eric began, "We . . . uh . . . thought you have been so good all week about going to bed that we wanted to come up and tuck you in again." Bobby had almost been asleep and he was still groggy. Pamela hugged him tightly for a second, Eric patted him on the head lovingly, and they said, "Goodnight." Bobby said, "Goodnight," and they left, shutting the door behind them. They walked silently downstairs into the living room, feeling a mixture of relief, sheepishness and anxiety about what might happen next.

They didn't have to wait long. Five minutes after they exited his room Bobby appeared at the threshold of the living room, blanket in tow, with a down-turned mouth and a wistful look in his eyes, staring at them. "What do you want, honey?" Pamela asked.

"Can I sit in your lap for a minute?" he whimpered.

"No, Bobby. It's past your bedtime. Get back up to bed," Eric said, trying to take charge.

"But I'm not tired," Bobby whined louder. "You guys woke me up and I'm not tired now!"

Pamela interjected, "Go on, honey. Back up to bed."

Bobby raised his voice and said, "I don't *want* to! And I don't have to!"

Eric's blood pressure shot up, he felt hot, and he glared

angrily at Pamela, rolling his eyes sarcastically as if to say that it was all her fault, and that if she weren't so sentimental this never would have happened.

Pamela felt Eric's contempt and shot back, "You're so damned passive-aggressive it's pathetic. Don't roll your eyes and make those sighing noises at *me!*"

As Bobby watched his parents fight, his eyes grew wider, his heart started pounding. As his anxiety heightened even more he shouted, "I want a glass of milk!"

Pamela turned toward Bobby and screamed at the top of her lungs, "You get back up to bed right now before I come over there and spank you so hard you won't be able to sit down for a week. Get up to bed!!! Now!!!" She charged toward him, blind with rage, her fist clenched and her arm raised, ready to strike. Eric screamed at her, "Pamela! Stop! You'll hurt him!" Pamela wheeled around on the balls of her feet to square off with Eric. On her way around, her eye caught a vase standing on a pedestal near the living room window. She lunged for it, pivoted a little more, raised it up and hurled it toward Eric. He ducked and the vase crashed violently against the wall, shattering into a thousand pieces. Bobby screamed and started to sob. Eric moved toward Pamela. Pamela stormed out of the house. Eric turned back to comfort Bobby, who was in a heap on the floor where he had stood moments ago. The house was eerily, achingly, silent except for the faint barking of the dog next door. Two blocks down the street, with tears pouring down her cheeks, Pamela sobbed, "Oh, God, please help us. It just *can't* go on this way. This is becoming monstrous."

The Beginning of Their Marriage

Pamela returned to the house thirty minutes later to find Bobby quietly in his room and Eric vacuuming up the last fragments of glass from the floor. They both feared the worst. They both felt like this was the beginning of the end of their marriage and family. They felt sick, lost, scared, empty, alone, confused and spent. The next day, they called to make an appointment and after they told us briefly what had happened we said that we wanted to see them for a session. When they entered our office, they looked miserable. We explained that we wanted to use half of the session to talk about what had happened the night before and half of the session to continue with their change program. They looked surprised. We were acting as if this were to be expected and that everything would work out okay.

Pamela described her violent rage. Eric described trying to intervene and the ensuing explosion. We listened patiently. After they had each described their experiences of the night before we took out the two flip chart pages containing their genograms and taped them back up on the easel. We asked Eric and Pamela to look at the genograms to see if they could detect any patterns that might help explain what happened, which they did. We explained that what had happened was a predictable step toward their becoming healthy adults. Our old patterns erupt in the present so that we can work them through and move beyond them. We explained that people unconsciously select a marital partner who will allow them to "bring forward their old wounds" so they can heal that part of themselves, allowing it to become "part of their best" rather than "part of their worst."

Eric jumped in and said, "So one of my childhood shortages is this fear of asserting myself, causing me to defer all the time. And this struggle with Bobby is giving me a chance to get in there and stand up for what I think is right."

Pamela added, "And I obviously need to move beyond what happened to me as a kid so I don't keep letting those old feelings dictate how I set limits with Bobby."

We agreed. They were beginning to move away from the guilt and shame from the night before while moving closer together as members of the same team. We explained that everyone has some pain from growing up and that to become a healthy adult we eventually need to make decisions based on what we know is right rather than on what our old feelings tell us. Pamela looked embarrassed when she said, "I *knew* we shouldn't have gone up to Bobby's room once he was settled for the night. But for a moment that old stuff came up from the darkness and I let it take over." "Yes," we replied. "This will happen from time to time. And part of your teamwork is to become increasingly aware of when it is happening, and then help each other stay on track."

"But what could we have done to avert this crisis in the first place?" Eric asked. "If we can't learn to do that, we're sunk." Pamela said that she wished Eric had stepped in and stopped her. Eric said that if he had, Pamela would have blown up at him. We asked him if he could handle her being mad at him for awhile. He thought for a moment and then said that he probably could, but he wouldn't like it. He then turned to Pamela and said, "Pamela, I just wish you'd get a grip. You've been spoiling Bobby since day one because you've wanted to undo your . . ."

As Pamela's face suddenly looked enraged, we abruptly said, "Eric, stop!" He stopped. We continued. "We want you to rephrase what you were saying but do it without shaming, blaming, finger-pointing or psychoanalyzing. What do you really want from Pamela in the future?"

He said, "Pamela, I will work on stepping in, as you have requested. What I'd like you to do is tell me when you're feeling like giving in to those feelings—signal me somehow."

Pamela's face softened and she said, "I can work on that, Eric. That would help me a lot just to know you want to hear what I'm feeling about this. Then I wouldn't feel so cut off and so alone with these feelings."

"Saying the feelings can take a lot of their power away," we said. "And sharing your feelings with each other—even the angry ones—will ultimately bring you together." They were getting it. They were beginning to recognize that the more separate they became, the closer they would be able to be. They were beginning to see that they each had their own issues with which to struggle and that no one could do that struggle for them. This is the process called "individuation." At the same time, they were beginning to see that they could be each others' allies in those struggles—they didn't have to deal with them in isolation. And then we asked them to say what they *appreciated* about their partner's childhood shortages, which threw them off for a moment.

Pamela finally said, "Eric, I really like your gentleness and desire to keep conflict down. That's one of the reasons I fell in love with you."

Eric said, "Pamela, I like the fact that you are so organized and so willing to make life fun for Bobby. You're a wonderful mother."

A few tears welled up in Pamela's eyes. "Oh, Eric," she began. "This isn't the end of our marriage. It's just the beginning."

Eric smiled and responded, "Isn't it amazing? The day after we thought it was all over is the day that it all just begins. We've needed to have this fight for a long time."

She said, "I know. It's been building. And we were both too scared to get it out until now. This feels so much better."

We then asked Eric and Pamela if they were ready to continue their important work of creating the new patterns that would serve them well for the rest of their parenting years. As hope replaced fear and shame in their countenances, they smiled warmly and said "Yes." We went over how the change program was working overall. We discussed the best way to pick up where they left off. They decided to briefly, and without fanfare, apologize to Bobby for going up to his room the night before, and to restate the bedtime that they'd put in place, and to thank him for doing such a good job up to this point.

Beyond Crisis

As you may have surmised, the preceding case description was condensed to be more readable. In some situations with some families the actual time elapsed from beginning through crisis to resolution may be several months, or even years, depending on how ready parents are to make changes. With some families, a crisis of this proportion never materializes. It all depends on what the partners brought into the relationship to begin with, how long the problem has gone unaddressed or unresolved, the presence of other crises and the strength of the marriage. This case description was also just a slice of what goes on as parents learn to apply behavior change programs with their kids. Especially in the early phases of the program, often a great deal of tinkering has to occur based on the child's unique reactions. Parents need to give themselves plenty of time to make a change program work, and they need to be as open, flexible and innovative as they can be. Where old patterns are deeply entrenched and intractable, outside support is extremely valuable, as is outside coaching from a professional.

And Remember

Bear in mind that the goal of a behavioral change program is not for you to become a dictator, but for you to have some reasonable structure and limits for your child so that both he and you can be healthy. The other goal is for you to learn to actually be in charge so that your child can feel safe. In many cases, perhaps the majority, once parents have instituted and consistently applied a new limit, such as a bedtime, their children take them more seriously when future limits are set because they know that manipulating won't be effective. That is why we can't encourage you enough to pick *one clear behavior* to change and then hold to that for several months before trying to change anything else. You aren't just enforcing a bedtime when you do that. You're also letting your child know that you are in charge of certain parts of his life and that no amount of posturing, bargaining, whining, tantrums or other manipulations will make any difference at all. In other words, you're taking your lives back and creating healthy marriages and healthy children in the process. Once you have accomplished that, the big crises with all the drama go away.

12

Some Final
Parenting Pointers

When it comes to self-improvement, we have found that if readers incorporate one or two tips into their lives then the book has been a success. This is especially true the more our readers are open to the serendipitous in life. Discovering unique patterns, principles or truths occurs most effectively when we are willing and able to "see" life from fresh perspectives. While the above statement may be circular, it is worth stating more than once because this kind of openness is the key to making lasting changes to the self. After all, the difference between trusting life and not trusting life isn't in how life manifests itself. It's in how we choose to interpret life's events as they unfold. If I am operating in the victim mode, I will see life as unfair, unsafe, cruel and malevolent. If I operate more as a competent adult, I will view life as exciting, challenging, painful at times, unfair at times and basically good.

With those thoughts in mind, we would like to complete this book with some general pointers that may be helpful to you, especially if you have not been able to apply any of the previous suggestions in this book. We would also like to remind you that you may not agree with everything we have written here, or with much of it at all. We simply ask that you be open to the possibility that there is a truth somewhere in this book that could make you a better parent. If you have read the book this far, you've probably already discovered it. If you haven't discovered it, then be open to the possibility that it is contained in one of the pointers described below.

The Eleven Best Things Parents Can Do

1. If Your Past Is in Your Way, Then by All Means Clear It Up

This may seem elementary, but it isn't. There is no such thing as a perfect childhood, and what's more, a lot of people who believe they had near-perfect childhoods actually had pretty flawed ones. We have worked with thousands of people who "knew" intellectually that they were not raising their children well because ghosts from their pasts were haunting them; nevertheless, they chose not to do anything about it because they were too afraid or ashamed. They expected their children to become adults when they hadn't become adults yet themselves. All of us, including the authors, do this to some degree. But if you keep tripping over your own past, please muster the courage to do something about it. Everyone has the courage to do this work. Clearing up your childhood ghosts isn't about blaming anyone it's about removing the blinders from your eyes so that you can stop being a prisoner of the automatic patterns you learned as a child.

In the early phase of this kind of work you may be angry about how you were treated or about the mistakes your parents made. But a competent therapist will help you identify those feelings and will then help you to reframe them in an adult perspective and move forward. That's the difference. The end result of that kind of work is not to remain angry. It is to find peace, acceptance, forgiveness where necessary, and then to move on into the rest of your life.

2. Talk with Others About Your Parenting Issues— If You Are Too Afraid or Ashamed, Then Force Yourself to Do It

One of the crucial differences between child batterers and those who do not batter is that nonbatterers are willing to talk to others about their parenting issues, and especially about their occasional feelings of desperation or hopelessness or anger while raising their kids. Talking about these most intimate, revealing feelings is what keeps us from acting them out. If you are too ashamed of those normal human feelings and, therefore, don't talk to anyone about them, then you may be a person who is at very high risk for battering your child.

Healthy parents discuss their parenting dilemmas and confusion with others. Some parents don't know how to do this, or where to find others with whom to talk. In that case, you have many options. You can call a local psychologist or mental health agency and ask if they know about parent support groups, or you can call The United Way, or a crisis hotline, or your church, or talk to your child's school counselor, or a neighbor; there are so many options.

3. Remember That There Are No Perfect Parents or Families or Children

Why is this important to remember? Because by keeping this fact in mind, you automatically take a lot of pressure off yourself to be perfect, which in turn takes a lot of pressure off your children, which in turn makes family life a lot more enjoyable. Some people get so ruffled about this because they still see everything in black and white. You either have to be perfect or you're a monster. That's an unfortunate view. There are a lot of spoiled kids out there, and there are a lot of abused kids out there, then there are a lot of really solid kids out there, and everything in between. The solid kids come from families where they are expected to become competent but where they are also expected to make mistakes, have fun and be confused at times.

Being a parent brings tremendous joy and, on occasion, heartache and sorrow. Being an adult means accepting that. It makes sense to say that being a competent, peaceful adult and being a good parent have much in common. So make room in your heart for your own shortcomings and also strive to become a better person as you go through your brief stay in this world. By keeping those in balance for yourself, you are very likely to keep them in balance for your children.

4. Your Children Are Not There to Raise You, Wait on You, Counsel You or Be Your Built-in Social Support

Your children need to have responsibilities, but not be slaves or little adults. If you don't have other adults in your life, find some. Some people say, "I don't have time to make new friends," or "I had a bad childhood and don't trust people," or "I wouldn't know where to begin to find friends," or "My children just love to stay home with me, and besides, it keeps them away from bad influences." But by leaning on your children for social support, you cripple them so that they can't grow up, which means they could end up living with you and living your life for you into their thirties, forties, fifties and beyond.

Should your children have chores to do? Of course they should. But if you selfishly expect them to wait on you hand and foot, and if you expect them to drop everything in their lives whenever you capriciously decide that you need them to help with chores, then we implore you to examine what you are doing to them and to yourself. Figure out what is reasonable to expect from children their age. Talk to others if you have no idea or if you suspect that what you did as a child was not reasonable. Then sit down with them and work up a system that they can go by and depend on. Take the lead on it. Make sure they follow through. And then leave them alone. Your kids need to do chores and participate in family life, but don't stop your son as he's heading out the door to his junior prom and tell him he can't go because you need him to help you wash the windows tonight. You don't need him for that right now even if you think you do.

5. Remember That One Small Change Held in Place Consistently Is Worth a Thousand Big Changes That Lack Follow-Through

That's all we need to say here. We've said it over and over throughout this book. Just remember it. Please.

6. If You Are Too Serious and Rigid, Learn to Loosen Up and Also Have Some Fun

Some people just don't know how to play and have fun, which is ultimately summarized in the credo, "Life's a bitch and then you die." Well, life is only a bitch most of the time if you make it so. It doesn't have to be. Many of us in this country have a hard time just having fun, being silly and not producing. There are so many serious, rigid people around that some very popular workshops teach people how to have fun and play.

Remember that control is good, and so is giving up control at times. It can be just fine if you don't get the lawn mowed perfectly this afternoon. It can be fun to sit around with a bunch of people after dinner, joking, laughing and talking. It might be worth experimenting with loosening up some of your rigid rules and conventions. The earth won't cease to rotate on its axis. The heavens won't open up and rain fire on you and all of your neighbors. Your son won't end up in prison if every once in awhile he gets a B or a C on his report card. It can be infinitely rewarding for you to let others see you being a real, comfortable, open human being.

7. If You Are Too Lax, Tighten Up

Some people are "by nature" less structured than others, as those of you who have ever taken the Myers-Briggs Type Indicator probably know. But being "less structured" is different than being too permissive or, worse, morally rudderless. Individuals lack structure in their lives for any number of reasons. Some are trying to overcompensate for a childhood of rigid, heartless, cruel rules and regulations. Others were raised to feel sorry for everyone and everything. Still others were so overprotected that they grew up actually believing that struggle is bad and that disappointment should be avoided at all cost.

Whatever the reason, if you now find that it literally breaks your heart to provide resistance for your children here and there, then please take a look at this. When children grow up without any resistance they begin to believe that there isn't any resistance in the universe, which leaves them incredibly unhappy and lost as they try, unsuccessfully, to enter adulthood and create their own life structure. We can't think of any situation in which this would be a functional way to raise a child.

8. Remember That When You Move from the Extremes into the Healthy Center, It Will "Feel Wrong"

If you tighten things up a bit after being too loose, you will feel like you are becoming mean. If you loosen up after being too tight, you will feel like you are becoming lax. Get input from others to confirm where you are on the continuum. Nobody knows how to handle every parenting situation flawlessly, but some people know how to handle some situations better than others. Look around. Watch. Listen. Be open. Finding the healthy middle ground is possible much of the time if you make that your goal. If you don't, you won't.

9. Examine Your Own Values and Lifestyle and Be Willing to Make Small, Effective Changes If Necessary

People can limit the amount of television they watch. It is possible to require everyone in the household to eat a couple of meals together each week. If you realize that your son has become hooked on computer games, don't sit around for months wringing your hands and getting into endless power struggles with him. This is like a rattlesnake bite. If you tend to it right away, you can avert much of the resulting illness and pain. If you don't, then you and your child suffer endless circular battles for years to come. Just do it. Remove the computer games from the computer's hard drive, and if that doesn't work, then move the computer to a room in the house where its use can be monitored properly, and then monitor it properly.

10. Show Leadership, Not Ownership

Don't be afraid to show leadership. Rather than being their owners, we are our children's guardians, their custodians and their guides. Remember that good leadership includes love, care and warmth, as well as structure and limits. It would appear that leadership is one of the more misunderstood concepts in American family life. We either act like tyrants or like our kids' best friends, neither of which is particularly helpful. A good leader inspires others to follow him or her.

Step back now and then and ask yourself what your example is inspiring your children to become. Are you inspiring them to have courage and determination or are you more an example of apathy and misery? Are you willing to make difficult personal decisions that are for the greater good and that will pay off in the long run, or are most of your decisions self-centered and short-sighted? Step back and see where you are leading your family, and by doing so, ensure that you can be proud of it rather than ashamed.

11. Don't Be Afraid to Experiment

Above all else, please take this to heart. Nobody ever gets anywhere without experimenting. No matter what your own personal "filters" tell you, children are astonishingly resilient. If you are feeling especially frustrated about a particular parenting dilemma, by all means try something different. Sometimes anything different is better than business as usual, even if the only thing you do differently is to drive home by a different route than you normally do. Changing an everyday routine can loosen up the unconscious just enough to allow you to generate new and effective solutions to really significant problems in your life, especially if you are also open to new ways of "seeing" the world.

If you are so rigid that you believe there is only one right way to do things, then get some help. This kind of rigidity creates problems that increase exponentially as your children get older because the farther out into life they go, the more there are multiple solutions to the same problem. An eighteen-month-old expresses her autonomy in pretty standard ways—by saying "no," by trying to toddle away from you, or by getting into things she's not supposed to. A twenty-five-year-old has many more avenues available to her for expressing autonomy—how she dresses, what career she chooses, her political beliefs, her religious beliefs, the company she keeps, where she chooses to live, what time she chooses to go to sleep at night, *ad infinitum*. If you still believe that there is only one right way to do things when your daughter is twenty-five, you are in for a lot of unnecessary heartache and conflict.

Being open to alternate solutions and being willing to experiment with your child-rearing methods and beliefs shows the kind of flexibility that will ultimately serve you and your children well. Life is not a test. You don't get graded every New Year's Eve. Life is to be lived as best we can, as creatively as we can, as fully as we can and as respectfully as we can. The same is true for our efforts as parents.

We hope you have benefited from reading this book, and we wish you all the best as you begin or continue one of the most rewarding journeys of anyone's life: *the journey through parenthood.*

REFERENCES

ABC News 20/20. August 8, 1997, Segment Two: "Pushover Parents." Produced by Penelope Fleming, edited by Mitch Udoff, and reported by Deborah Roberts. To purchase a copy of this segment, contact ABC News at 1-800-CALL ABC.

Arnold, K., and T. Denny. Study of Illinois high school valedictorians cited in D. Goleman, *Emotional Intelligence,* New York: Bantam, 1995.

Bateson, G. "The Cybernetics of Self: A Theory of Alcoholism." *Psychiatry* 34 (1971): 1.

Berg, S. "The New Simplicity Movement." *Minneapolis StarTribune,* December 1997.

Bouchard, T. J., Jr., David T. Lykken, M. McGue, N. Segal, and A. Tellegen. "Sources of Human Psychological Differences: The Minnesota Study of Twins Reared Apart." *Science,* 12 October 1990: 223–228.

Brown, H. Jackson, Jr. *A Father's Book of Wisdom.* Nashville: Rutledge Hill Press, 1988.

Bruner, J. S. "The Course of Cognitive Growth." *American Psychologist* 19 (1964): 1–14.

Doherty, W. *The Intentional Family: How to Build Family Ties in Our Modern World.* New York: Addison-Wesley, 1997.

Erikson, E. H. *Identity: Youth and Crisis.* New York: W. W. Norton & Co., 1968.

Gibran, K. *The Prophet.* New York: Alfred A. Knopf, 1982.

Goleman, D. *Emotional Intelligence: Why It Can Matter More Than IQ.* New York: Bantam, 1995.

Greeley, A. Cited in "Talking to God: An Intimate Look at the Way We Pray." *Newsweek,* 6 January 1992.

Kagan, J. *Galen's Prophecy.* New York: Basic Books, 1994.

Kagan, J. "Reflectivity-Impulsivity: The Generality and Dynamics of Conceptual Tempo." *Journal of Abnormal Psychology* 71 (1966): 17–24.

Kohlberg, L., J. Yaeger, and E. Hjertholm. "Private Speech: Four Studies and a Review of Theories." *Child Development* 39 (1968): 691–736.

Lao-tzu. *Tao Te Ching.* Feng, G. F., and J. English, trans. New York: Random House, 1972.

Loevinger, J. *Ego Development: Conceptions and Theories.* San Francisco: Jossey-Bass, 1977.

Louis-Harris Poll. *USA Today,* 27 February 1998.

Luria, A. R. "The Directive Function of Speech in Development and Dissolution." *Word* 15 (1959): 351–352.

Maddock, J. W., and Noel R. Larson. *Incestuous Families: An Ecological Approach to Understanding and Treatment.* New York: W. W. Norton, 1995.

McNeill, D. "The Development of Language." In *Carmichael's Manual of Child Psychology,* edited by P. H. Mussen. 3rd ed. New York: John Wiley & Sons, Inc., 1970.

Meichenbaum, D. H. "The Nature and Modification of Impulsive Children: Training Impulsive Children to Talk to Themselves." *Research Report,* no. 23 (10 April 1971), Department of Psychology, University of Waterloo, Waterloo, Ontario, Canada.

Milgram, S. "Behavioral Study of Obedience." *Journal of Personality and Social Psychology* 67 (1963): 371–378.

Mischel, W. "Theory and Research on the Antecedents of Self-Imposed Delay of Reward." In *Progress in Experimental Personality Research,* vol. 3, edited by B. A. Maher. New York: Academic Press, 1966.

Ornish, D. *Love and Survival: The Scientific Basis for the Healing Power of Intimacy.* New York: HarperCollins, 1998.

Ornish, D. *Dr. Dean Ornish's Program for Reversing Heart Disease.* New York: Random House, 1990.

Paloma and Gallup. Statistics cited in "Talking to God: An Intimate Look at the Way We Pray." *Newsweek,* 6 January 1992.

Piaget, J. *The Origin of Intelligence in Children.* New York: International Universities Press, 1936.

Pipher, M. *The Shelter of Each Other: Rebuilding Our Families.* New York: Grosset/Putnam, 1996.

Rimm, S. *Smart Parenting: How to Parent so Children Will Learn.* New York: Three Rivers Press, 1996.

Satir, V. *Conjoint Family Therapy.* Palo Alto: Science and Behavior Books, 1967.

Schnarch, D. *Passionate Marriage: Sex, Love, and Intimacy in Emotionally Committed Relationships.* New York: W. W. Norton, 1997.

Shoda, Y., W. Mischel, and P. K. Peake. "Predicting Adolescent Cognitive and Self-Regulatory Competencies from Preschool Delay of Gratification." *Developmental Psychology* 26, no. 6 (1990): 978–986.

Vaillant, G. *Adaptation to Life.* Boston: Little, Brown, 1977.

Vygotsky, L. S. *Thought and Language.* Cambridge: MIT Press, 1962.

INDEX

185

ABOUT THE AUTHORS

John C. Friel, Ph.D., and Linda D. Friel, M.A., are licensed psychologists in private practice in New Brighton, Minnesota, a suburb of St. Paul. They have three grown children who have left the nest, and a female Labrador retriever and a male cockapoo who live at home with them. The Friels do individual, couple and family therapy and ongoing men's and women's therapy groups as well as seminars and workshops in America, Canada, England and Ireland, for the general public, hospitals, corporations, universities, mental health clinics and government agencies. They also conduct the Clearlife/Lifeworks Clinic in several U.S. locations. The Clinic is a gentle three-and-a-half day process designed to help participants discover old patterns that are tripping them up in the present, and to begin to create new patterns that are healthier.

They are the bestselling authors of *Adult Children: The Secrets of Dysfunctional Families; An Adult Child's Guide to What's "Normal"; The Grown-Up Man: Heroes, Healing,*

Honor, Hurt, Hope; Rescuing Your Spirit; and *The Soul of Adulthood: Opening The Doors.*

They can be contacted by mail at:

Friel Associates/ClearLife/Lifeworks
P.O. Box 120148
New Brighton, MN 55112-0013
phone: 651-628-0220
fax: 612-904-0340
(please note the two different area codes for phone and fax)

Their Web site, which includes books, tapes, speaking schedules and a monthly column written by their two dogs, Minnesota Sam and Abby, can be located at: *www.clearlife.com.*

New for Kids

Chicken Soup for the Kid's Soul

Jack Canfield, Mark Victor Hansen, Patty Hansen and Irene Dunlap

Young readers will find empowerment and encouragement to love and accept themselves, believe in their dreams, find answers to their questions and discover hope for a promising future.

Code 6099, $12.95

Chicken Soup for the Teenage Soul II

Jack Canfield, Mark Victor Hansen and Kimberly Kirberger

The stories in this collection will show teens the importance of friendship, family, self-respect, dreams, and life itself.

Code 6161, $12.95

Chicken Soup for the Teenage Soul Journal

Jack Canfield, Mark Victor Hansen and Kimberly Kirberger

This personal journal offers teens the space to write their own life stories, as well as space for their friends and parents to offer them words of love and inspiration.

Code 6374, $12.95

The New Kid and the Cookie Thief

Story adaptation by Lisa McCourt
Illustrated by Mary O'Keefe Young

For a shy girl like Julie, there couldn't be anything worse than the very first day at a brand new school. What if the kids don't like her? What if no one ever talks to her at all? Julie's big sister has some advice—and a plan—that just might help. But will Julie be too scared to even give it a try?

Code 5882, hardcover, $14.95

Available in bookstores everywhere or call 1-800-441-5569 for Visa or MasterCard orders.
Prices do not include shipping and handling. Your response code is **BKS.**

This collection captures the essence of being a woman, with true stories about love, attitude, marriage, friendship, overcoming obstacles and achieving dreams. This book will help women gain balance and a new perspective on life, and renew their faith in the human spirit.

Code 6226 • $12.95

Available in bookstores everywhere or call 1-800-441-5569 for Visa or MasterCard orders. Prices do not include shipping and handling.
Your response code is BKS.

The Parent's Little Book of Lists

This is a handy reference with practical, kid-tested ideas to help parents deal with everything from monsters in the closet to unsolicited criticism of parenting abilities.
Code 5122, quality softcover, $10.95

Parents, Teens and Boundaries

How parents set boundaries with their teens is one of the most important aspects of the parent-child relationship. Jane Bluestein looks at twenty aspects of boundary-setting and clearly explains when to set boundaries and how to express and maintain them.

Code 2794, quality softcover, $8.95

Safeguarding Your Teenager from the Dragons of Life

Bettie Youngs shows us how to keep teenagers on track toward worthwhile goals by providing the support they need to become responsible, happy adults.
Code 2646, quality softcover, $11.95

More from John & Linda Friel

Adult Children

This book defines the problems of dysfunctional families. Combining theory
and clinical practice, this book provides
an explanation of what happened and
how to rectify it.
Code 0-932194-53-2,
quality softcover, $8.95

An Adult's Guide to What's "Normal"

Recovery for adults who grew up in
troubled homes isn't as simple as it
may appear. This book offers concise
strategies for escaping these traps.
Code 0902, quality softcover, $9.95

The Soul of Adulthood

Adulthood is a quality of soul that is
chosen and earned through the very
deepening struggles that life kindly
offers us as we progress from birth to
death. The Friels guide us to the deeper
realms of our souls.
Code 3413, $9.95